THE DOLLARS AND SENSE OF HONESTY

The Dollars and Sense of Honesty

Stories from the Business World

GEORGE D. ARMERDING

with PHIL LANDRUM

1817

Published in San Francisco by HARPER & ROW, PUBLISHERS

New York, Hagerstown, San Francisco, London

*Dedicated to those business people
whose ethical standards excel
in the world of commerce.*

THE DOLLARS AND SENSE OF HONESTY:
Stories from the Business World. Copyright © 1979 by
George D. Armerding and Phil Landrum. All rights
reserved. Printed in the United States of America. No
part of this book may be used or reproduced in any
manner whatsoever without written permission except
in the case of brief quotations embodied in critical
articles and reviews. For information address Harper &
Row, Publishers, Inc., 10 East 53rd Street, New York,
N.Y. 10022. Published simultaneously in Canada by
Fitzhenry & Whiteside, Limited, Toronto.

FIRST EDITION

Designed by Jim Mennick

Library of Congress Cataloging in Publication Data

Armerding, George D.
  THE DOLLARS AND SENSE OF HONESTY.

  1. Business ethics. I. Landrum, Phil, joint au-
thor. II. Title.
HF5387.A73 1979 174'.4 77-7854
ISBN 0-06-060301-1

79 80 81 82 83 10 9 8 7 6 5 4 3 2 1

Contents

Introduction

THE ACCEPTED standards whereby one person does business with another have changed radically in the past quarter century. Business people seem to be coasting along on the impetus supplied by God-fearing generations of the past—but that force is gradually fading out. Efforts to raise the standards in the business community are either misdirected or totally lacking. Spiritual codes have degenerated into moral codes and moral codes have been corrupted by a lowering of the true sense of values.

Biblical standards for commerce have been replaced with legal statutes by politicians under duress from highly paid lobbyists. And equally effective, well-rewarded legal counsel is being retained to circumvent those laws. The profit incentive is the driving force that keeps the whole process motivated. The genuine, true spirituality that should control our morals has given way to materialism.

There are those who are seeking to reverse this trend. They are alarmed at the destruction of our environment and the depletion of our national resources. Their aim is to protect what remains and restore, if possible, that which has been destroyed. There are apparently no organizations in existence or even being formed whose aim is to restore high standards in the world of commerce. This would normally be the function of the church. Strangely, though, the church has remained aloof of its responsibility in this area. Unless a renaissance begins with the spiritual community, the hope for improvement seems dim.

The purpose of this volume is twofold. First, it provides a profile of experiences from the business community of the nation that point out the dangers in the present situation. Second, by revealing and exposing our weaknesses and failures, it indicates a hope that a solution to the problem might become evident. We need to establish confidence in our fellows whether they be politicians, business people, clergy, social connections or day-to-day contacts.

The improvement must begin with the individual. The question is not "How much can I get away with?" but rather "How much can I do to improve my own objectives?" Materialism should no longer be the impelling force. Self-improvement can only follow spiritual growth. The overall correction of our national problems must begin with the Christian community.

It is the desire and purpose of the authors, as well as of the contributors, that this volume will ignite a spark in the heart of each reader that will light the torch to guide us through the darkness that has enveloped us and blinded our vision.

Part One

THE ETHICS SITUATION: IS IT REALLY THAT BAD?

CHAPTER 1

The Ethics
Slide

JUDDY'S FIRST JOB

Juddy had just finished his first year at college and desperately needed a summer job. He wasn't particular, but his first efforts came up empty until someone suggested that he try the local freight office.

The agent was very sympathetic and offered Juddy a job checking boxcars for demurrage, a fee charged for cars held over a limited period.

"Just what do I have to do on that job?"

"Well, do you know your way around this town?"

"Yes," Juddy replied. "I've lived here for some six years. I think I know most of the business places."

"Your job is to check the freight cars on every siding. You live near the edge of town and can begin there right after you leave home. Then work your way along both sides of the track clear across to the other side of town."

The agent then detailed the job responsibilities. It sounded good to Juddy and he began his work the very next day with high hopes.

The job was demanding but each day Juddy improved. Within a week he was able to check all his stops in about five hours.

Juddy was surprised at the reaction of the other employees.

"Not checking in already, are you Juddy?"

"Sure, I think in another week or so I'll be through with the route by noontime."

"Listen, Juddy, get wise. That job is a full-day job. If you want to avoid serious trouble you better not report in here much before quitting time."

"Oh, I couldn't do that," Juddy replied. "I just couldn't loaf along like that."

"If you know what's good for your health you will. Now get out of here and don't come back until we're ready to lock up for the day."

Juddy left the office confused. His father had taught him always to give an honest day's work for an honest day's pay. He wandered along the railroad tracks trying to figure it out.

Several days later he got another jolt from one of the customers of the railroad. As he walked up to a boxcar on the siding a fellow called out to him.

"Hey, kid, you needn't check that car. It's all unloaded."

Juddy was close enough to see that the car was still partially filled with cases of merchandise.

"It doesn't look empty to me."

"Don't worry about that. It will be by the time the switch engine gets here this afternoon. Late charges are very expensive. I don't want to have to pay for an extra day on account of just a few cases. Mark in your book that the car was empty and run along."

Juddy walked away but as he strolled to the next siding he made a notation in his book, "partially unloaded." He was actually scared. What would happen when the customer got the bill for the demurrage charges?

Before the week was over Juddy faced still another problem. His education in the world of commerce was getting pretty rough. As he approached the siding of a local manufacturing company, the switching crew was just coming out of the yard. They had placed an empty boxcar for loading. The engine stopped before going on to the main line and the conductor called to Juddy, "Don't check that car in until tomorrow. The guy who runs that plant is a buddy of mine."

"But, I have to account for every car," replied Juddy. "If I don't show it here the number will have to appear in another location."

"Show it on the station siding," the conductor yelled back as the switch engine pulled away.

Now Juddy was having trouble sleeping.

Was every job in industry like this? Does everybody cheat? The questions went unanswered. Then the agent called Juddy into his office.

"Juddy," the agent said, "you checked a car at the customer's siding as partially unloaded. We charged him demurrage. He is screaming about the bill and says the car was empty that day. How about it?"

Juddy told him the whole story and then added,

"While I'm talking to you I might just as well tell you a few more things. That job of mine is not really a full-time job. I could finish checking those sidings by noon everyday but I was warned not to come in much before quitting time. I don't like to loaf on the job and I don't want to be dishonest either. I just cannot go on working like this. It isn't the way I was brought up. However, I don't want to lose my job either."

Juddy's story had a happy ending. He got a promotion. But, he also may have gotten fired.

THE ETHICS OF BUSINESS

Juddy's experience is certainly not unusual. But, why? I see three main reasons: (1) the ethics slide, (2) the circumventers, and (3) the profit incentive.

We are in the midst of an ethics slide. The standards whereby one person does business with another have changed radically. We're coasting along on the impetus supplied by God-fearing generations of the past.

However, that force is gradually fading out.

Efforts to raise the standards in the business community are either misdirected or totally lacking. Spiritual codes of ethics have degenerated into moral codes. Moral codes have been corrupted by a lowering of the true sense of values.

Biblical standards for commerce have been replaced with legal statutes by politicians under duress from highly paid lobbyists.

Equally effective, well-rewarded legal counsel is being retained to circumvent the laws.

The profit incentive is the driving force that keeps the whole process motivated. The genuine, true spirituality that controls our morals has given way to materialism.

There are apparently no organizations in existence or even being formed whose aim is to restore high standards in the conduct of commerce. Even the church has remained aloof of its responsibility in this area. Agencies strive to save the redwoods. Others guard against destruction of endangered species. Where are the agencies to raise ethical standards in business? Unless a renaissance begins with the spiritual community, the hopes for improvement seem dim.

WHERE DID IT ALL START?

Where did it all start—the matter of business ethics?

Possibly the first recorded business transaction in history is found in the Bible, a deal worked out between the patriarch Abraham and a man named Ephron.

Abraham left Babylon with his wife Sarah to migrate into the land of Palestine, only to have Sarah die when they reached Hebron.

Abraham had a problem. The family burial plot was located back in Mesopotamia. Too far to take his wife's body. He needed a place to bury her.

Ephron owned a field with a cave that would make an ideal burial place. The transaction was a simple one. No zoning ordinances were involved in that transaction. There were no title companies to deal with, no ecology committees to be appeased. It was simply a matter of paying the owner his price and taking possession. After a bit of bargaining they completed the deal.

Times have changed considerably since then. Today, such a transaction would involve agencies, brokers, permits, and restrictions, not to mention the capital gains tax that Ephron would have to pay.

The simple transaction of the past has become a complex

problem requiring legal counsel and involving a host of regulations that the average person never heard of and cannot understand. The details are costly and inconvenient. So, there is a tendency to seek a way around the obstacles rather than to conform to the requirements.

Some shortcuts seem insignificant. Others involve all sorts of schemes and nefarious devices to save time, money, and work.

"MR. FIXIT"

Some people are proud of their ability to ferret out every loophole and still remain within the confines of the law. They recommend this sort of procedure to their friends.

"No problem—I'm not suggesting that you break any laws. Why suffer and pay out all those additional funds when you don't have to." Sounds reasonable. It's tempting to follow this course.

"People have created the problems. Why shouldn't other people figure out ways to get around the problems? It's good business. Be sharp and take advantage of every means you can to save time and expense while remaining within the confines of the law."

This "business on the edge" has an effect, though.

Principles and conscience are sacrificed on the altar of big business. It's easier than ever to slip from poor ethical behavior into illegal activities. The erosion or slippage in principles is so gradual that we are completely unaware of the change in our moral standards. In fact, we soon become amoral people with seared consciences.

Turning to a person who is going to save you money can

ultimately lead to your turning for everything to a "Mr. Fixit" complete with a list of payoff fees for everyone.

THE EFFECTS

Wrong business practices and methods sooner or later affect everyone in the marketplace. Minor infractions of the rules are no longer frowned upon, but accepted as a way of life.

We shield ourselves from criticism with, "Everybody is doing it."

Things once considered unethical have crept into the category of normal accepted business standards. "If there is no law against it, why be concerned about it?" Moral responsibility is no longer relevant.

Good people tend toward shortcuts.

Good people—like Joe.

Joe managed a large grain elevator. He believed in doing the right thing all the time. Yet, when he loaded out a car of No. 2 corn, he blended in some "sample grade" corn. Nothing wrong with that.

Just as long as the final product didn't exceed the moisture content of the No. 2 grade. It didn't bother him that the "sample grade" might get moldy and cause a lot of damage later on. He was making a bit more money for his company. That was his real duty.

This reasoning is normal in, today's business world. With narrow margins of profit, a good manager seeks out and takes advantage of every percentage point. Society praises this kind of person—it doesn't condemn.

"A shrewd businessman with cold water in his veins," we say.

THE ETHICS SLIDE STARTS SMALL

Countless little things today are basically wrong. They seem of little value so they are never challenged.

Since there is no penalty—not even a rebuke—the little things grow larger, more serious.

Such trends are difficult to reverse. Trivial indiscretions lead to downright transgressions. Soon, people with high standards become color-blind to the blinking red lights of conscience compromising and are swept along with those who never had very high ethical standards in the first place.

The business person enters the gray zone of business practices, soon inventing or using a series of alibis.

"No one will be harmed by what I am doing. Everyone is doing the same thing. There is no law against it. I'm entitled to my share. The rules are too strict and impractical. No one can operate at a profit without cutting a few corners. If I don't do it I'll probably lose my job. It's a trivial matter, not worth an argument."

The result of listening to this rationalization? Eventually, we lose our sense of values. We are not even aware that this sense is slipping away from us.

AMOS'S MILK POWDER

Amos managed a large cooperative dairy plant that produced, among other things, a large quantity of spray-dried milk solids. This product sold for a much higher price than milk dried on a roller dryer.

Amos got an idea to increase profits. He purchased the cheaper roller-dried product on the open market. Then he constructed a hopper with an automatic feeder that introduced about five pounds of the cheap powder with each ninety-five pounds of the expensive powder.

This operation cost little but increased earnings considerably.

One day a friend walked through the plant and noticed the operation. He challenged Amos, who had an excellent reputation in the community.

"Amos, I'm surprised to see you blending roller powder in with the spray powder."

"Oh, that's OK. It's all milk powder. No one will ever know the difference."

"You know," the friend replied, "the roller powder is not very soluble. It will affect your solubility index."

"Not that little bit. We're only putting in five percent."

"Supposing a government inspector catches you?"

"How would he?" Amos asked.

"Let's take some of that blended powder and look at it under a microscope."

They placed some of the powder on a slide. The particles of the spray-dried milk powder were smooth with no sharp edges. The cheaper powder had been run through a mill to break it up. Each particle had sharp edges.

"Anyone could tell the difference and would know at once that you had cheated them."

Amos was convinced. He quit the moneymaking scheme that had looked so good to him. Not because of his conscience but because he thought he might get caught.

IF I DIDN'T SOMEBODY ELSE WOULD

Mac owned a printing plant. One of his presses was turning out a brochure reporting on missionary activity in Zaire. A short distance away a full color machine was producing posters for an X-rated movie.

A visitor to the plant watched the operation for a few moments. Turning to the printer he asked, "How come, Mac? Doesn't your conscience bother you when you turn out stuff like that right alongside something so deeply religious?"

"Oh no. Doesn't make a bit of difference to me. If I didn't print it someone else would. The profit margin on that job is four times greater than what we will make on the brochure. I might just as well do it and pick up a few extra dollars."

GEORGE SAVES MONEY

George was a laboratory technician in a large fresh-food plant. His job was quality control. However, sales had fallen. Drivers were bringing back huge quantities of the product—returns that represented potentially great losses.

George came up with an idea. Why not launder the product, add some ingredients to bring it up to standard, and run it through a separator. Quality would be back to "normal." Presto! Fresh food. George perfected a way of doing this. It was so subtle he could do it while the health inspector was in the plant at the time.

"What you are doing is not very ethical, George," suggested a friend. "You're fooling buyers into thinking they are getting fresh food. Is that right?"

"Of course. This product is superior to the stuff they're getting from our competitors."

He didn't change his procedure.

The people in these illustrations are all reputable pillars in their society; they are accepted as having high ethical principles.

The examples show how ethical standards can erode gradually and subtly.

When confronted, each remained unconvinced he was doing anything truly wrong. They were unaware of the change in their conduct over a few brief years.

THE RESULTS

Have we Americans abandoned our ethical and religious traditions? Are we solely occupied with material gains, losing sight of human values? Is the average person more concerned with how much he can get rather than how much he can give? If this is the present state of our society, we need to reexamine our philosophy of life and its purpose.

A review of history will teach us that nations of the past crumbled under similar circumstances. A continual craving for more has contributed to our downward course.

To reverse the trend and restore the high moral and ethical principles upon which the nation was founded will take the combined effort of every individual in our land. The initial steps of leadership should come from the Christian Business Person. Not those who call themselves Christians and are not, but those who do not need to wear their religion on their sleeves. The Christian with high ethical and moral principles must supply the leadership so sorely needed.

The book "Profiles in Courage" tells stories of how politicians stood in the gap at key points in history.

The current slide cannot be ignored by any Christian Business Person. Future generations will look back at us with scorn and derision and say, "These were the people who had it within their power to save the nation but failed." Or they may point with pride to their ancestors who reversed the trend and restored the nation to its original high standard of integrity.

The purpose of this volume is twofold. First, it provides a profile of experiences from the business community of the nation to point out the danger areas in the present situation. Second, by revealing or exposing our weaknesses and failures, it indicates a hope that a solution to the problem will become evident. We need to reestablish confidence in our ethics whether they involve politics, business, the pulpit, our social life, or our day-to-day contacts with each other.

The improvement must begin with the individual. The question is not "How much can I get away with?" but rather "how much can I do to improve my objectives?"

Materialism should no longer be the impelling force.

Self-improvement can only follow spiritual growth. The overall correction of our national problems must begin with the Christian community.

CHAPTER 2

"We're Number One"

ATTITUDE CHECK

Feeding the ethics slide are some basic attitudes that have become a way of life in our world.

Let's consider three.

We're No. One

This is the most obvious contribution to the ethics slide.

Covetousness in its highest form is undoubtedly the impelling force that drives a person or an enterprise to become "Number One." No cost is too great, no sacrifice is too costly to bring about the desired result, the mysterious goal.

It is the lodestone of industry, the will-o'-the-wisp of sports, beckoning the contender on to an invisible goal, presumably just a step ahead of the nearest competitor.

The desire for this supposed pinnacle of fame is not limited to just a few ambitious organizations. The idea of being "Number One" has influenced BIG corporations, nations, football and baseball teams, golfers, race car drivers, and a host of others to spend huge sums or exert supreme effort to acquire the title.

Striving to become "Number One" is older than civilization. Satan himself had this ambition when he said,

"I am a god, I sit in the seat of God." This desire cost him dearly.

Being "Number One" sent the explorers scooting to all parts of the globe.

Marco Polo started it by journeying across Asia to visit the great Kubla Khan. This began the era of exploration.

Portugal sent Vasco da Gama around the bottom of Africa to find a water route to the Indies. Magellan sailed westward through the dangerous straits that now bear his name.

The British sent Henry Hudson, Martin Frobisher, George Vancouver, and others on similar journeys. They had Francis Drake, John Cabot, and James Cook prowling the seas in search of the shortest way to the land where spices grew. They wanted to be "Number One."

The same thrill of a chase to be first sent Richard Burton, David Livingstone, Henry Morton Stanley, and others off looking for the source of the Nile in Central Africa.

When Alexander the Great got to be "Number One" he wept because there were no more worlds to conquer. He died a mere youth. But his successes inspired the Romans to go on a similar spree. They got to be "Number One." Where are they now?

The satisfaction of being on top is short-lived. Everybody seems to be gunning for the fellow on top. Ball teams schedule their best pitchers to meet the league leaders. Basketball and football teams get all keyed up to upset the team in front. Still the quest goes on.

World wars have been fought so a nation could be "Number One." The result? Millions of lives sacrificed.

The Russians hurled their sputnik into orbit around the world. They were "Number One." And a frantic Congress urged on by a zealous president voted billions so we could be first to put a man on the moon. Watergate was a result of this philosophy.

Is this quest, which precedes civilization, worth it? Should we sacrifice our ethics, morals, and sterling principles to it? Is being "Number One" worth the cost? What does it do for the folks who make it? Feed their ego, I am sure, but what else? Unfortunately, wanting to be "Number One" has encouraged us to make shortcuts a way of life.

Materialism: Blessing or Curse?

Materialism is the second attitude contributing to the ethics slide. A materialist is more concerned with the physical realm than with the intellectual or spiritual parts of life.

Materialism can be both a blessing and a curse.

Materialism is the lifeblood of industry, the dynamic force that keeps the wheels of progress turning. It is the urge that makes people run their businesses at a profit and their bodies at a loss.

It is the demagogue that demands two wage earners in every family. It puts the homemaker into the rat race of commerce. It creates the moonlighter.

Materialism makes everyone resent what he lacks more than appreciate what he has. It is the pressure that keeps the gross national product figure climbing over the trillion mark. It reduces art to a science and science to a production line monster.

Materialism is also the barrage that brings life-giving water to a thirsty desert making it bloom like a rose. It is the hybridization of plants to make five sacks of rice grow where only one grew before. It is the conservancy that prevents the erosion of valuable land. It is the rehabilitation agency that cleans up slums and provides desirable housing instead.

Materialism is also a doctrine that has remade the church into an establishment and transformed the minister into an ecclesiastical news commentator. It has taken worship out of the realm of the spiritual and put it into the imaginary belt of the zodiac. It has replaced the fear of the Divine with the influence of the stars.

Materialism is the political magician who can squeeze a whole precinct into a voting machine. It is the mother of new nations born in a day. It is the cartographer who pushes national boundaries two hundred miles out to sea. It is the lobbyist who lurks in the halls of every legislature.

Materialism depletes natural resources and destroys the environment. It degrades wilderness areas into litter-strewn acres. It drives wild life closer and closer to extinction. It is the modern construction engineer who diverts a thundering waterfall into a power plant. It scars our cities with double- and triple-decked superhighways. It replaces historic structures with twentieth-century high-rise cliff dwellings. It churns a placid lake into a water skiers paradise.

Materialism turns amateurs into pros and changes sports into a commercial enterprise. It transforms the home into a theatre interspersed with commercials in full color. It has the unique ability to convert personalities into a series of digits. It is a news medium that headlines tragedy and confines good news to a two-column, three-inch block.

Materialism is an arms race that piles up a tremendous deficit and keeps the caldrons of international stew boiling. It is a space program that puts people on the moon and sends vehicles probing the secrets of the planets. It is a sophisticated laboratory spawning new products that render obsolete those born yesterday.

Materialism is a computerized conglomerate that gobbles up healthy little entrepreneurs. It makes every profession a team of specialists and elevates the garbage collector to an ecology engineer. It keeps the semanticist hunting for bigger and more explosive words for the ad writer.

Materialism is the charm that seduces even the skeptic. It is a hunger never satisfied, a thirst never quenched. It takes the leisure and the tedium out of travel.

Materialism synthesizes the natural and reduces its value to pennies. It is the scoundrel who uses beautiful flowers to produce dope addicts. It creates a din that drowns out the sweet sounds of nature.

Materialism is the numismatic fiend who takes silver coins out of circulation and buries them in deep, dark, secret places. It is the criminal who hijacks a cargo and pushes insurance rates into orbit. It is the mother of litigation that crowds the courts with damage suits that wax fatter and fatter with each succeeding judgment.

The biblical admonition to prove all things and hold fast to that which is good must be applied to materialism.

On Demand

Attitude three: the demands we make on one another.

Surely one of the most resented words in the English

language is the word *demand.* It carries real authority but causes our ire to rise when an irrevocable imperative is directed our way. We could improve relationships by making our requests in a milder manner.

But no.

Unions present industry with their demands. Demonstrators march with placards to publicize their demands. Lawsuits are being filed by the hundreds and thousands with seemingly endless demands. Minority groups threaten with demands.

THE CHRISTIAN BUSINESS PERSON

The Christian business person shouldn't be characterized by a threatening attitude. What quality should he display in his dealings with his fellows? Certainly one of forebearance and leniency. It should be his desire to refrain from extracting the last drop of blood or the pound of flesh.

Consider the alternative.

Insurance costs skyrocket due to previously unheard of claims. Doctors and hospitals carry expensive insurance coverage as a result of the extravagant claims settlements allowed by judges and juries. No one is exempt. Everyone is vulnerable.

Politicans explain their generosity with the excuse that the public is demanding more and more. The constituency demands it. Otherwise, there will be a new representative or senator next time.

Employers demand more from employees. Employees demand higher pay, more fringe benefits, shorter working hours, and longer vacations.

Farmers demand bigger government subsidies. Manufacturers ask the government for higher import duties or lower quotas to reduce competition from other nations.

Everyone is demanding. Not all the demands can be met. Yet, such is the trend of our times. Can equitable practices survive in the light of such demands—especially when it is even hard to know what is equitable anymore?

A NEW DEFINITION FOR ETHICS

Dictionary editors may have to revise the definition of the word *ethics*. It is no longer a rigid inflexible set of moral principles or values dealing with what is good and what is bad. There are now gray areas. Therefore, the definition must be modified to include some form of compromise.

It may be considered ethical for a prominent government leader to accept $1,000 for making a mediocre speech but very unethical to accept a gift of a vicuna coat.

The United States Senate has established that it is ethical to earn so much each year by moonlighting, but to earn $1 more a year would be unethical.

Ethics has become a matter of geography. To purchase favors from overseas buyers should not really be classed as wrongdoing for this has been the accepted custom down through the centuries. To resort to the same tactics at home, however, would be very much out of order. Certain restraints apply within the borders of the nation, but anything outside of those boundaries comes under a different set of rules and is acceptable.

A fund-raising organization may argue vehemently that costs are not out of line even if two-thirds or more of the contributions received are used to cover operating costs. Another group may pride itself in keeping expenses below ten percent of the total gifts received while still a third agency may frown on holding back as much as a dollar.

The manufacturer of an unusual or highly specialized piece of equipment may price it for all the traffic will bear rather than at cost plus a reasonable profit.

The doctor may extend the patient's treatment far beyond what is necessary since Medicare, Blue Cross, or some other insurance plan will pick up the tab. Superfluous tests or X rays may be made simply to provide protection for the physician against some future legal action.

Unmarried couples find nothing wrong in living together to reduce the combined amount of their taxes.

An airline company has no qualms about cancelling a flight because of "equipment difficulties." The real reason? Not enough passengers or mail to make a profitable flight.

A merchant advertises a "50% off" sale. The buyer finds that this includes only a few of the special sizes that did not sell well.

A lawyer brings a case for damages into court since his fee is far greater than it would have been had the matter been settled across his office desk.

The list is endless. Such practices are generally expected. Is this ethics?

No.

Ethics is not a man-made set of rules for living. A mere man cannot put together a guide for conduct superior to that we already have in the Bible. Any effort to improve it would destroy it.

Humanity's codes and the Scriptures have been more often divorced than married. A Christian must find answers in God's Word. Then he must allow these standards to control his conduct and dictate the rules for living.

This is the best place to check out attitudes—and make sure we're not contributing to the ethics slide.

CHAPTER 3

The Downward
Pull

ERODING ETHICS

The business person who embarks on a course geared to the ethics of the Bible cannot expect an easy trip.

He must expect that what he thinks is bad ethics will be considered standard practice by some fellow business people.

He must realize that what he considers normal will be considered abnormal by others.

Is this negative thinking?

No. It is merely dealing with the negative. And dealing with the negative in order to correct it is positive.

It is much like the doctor who deals with the illness to produce a positive result.

It is like the lifesaver who practices for hours against the most extreme conditions (wild, panicky "victims" in lifesaving classes throwing the most unreasonable tactics imaginable at him) so that he is ready when faced with that potentially fatal moment.

Just because he knows he might some day face a wild, panicky victim—and is prepared for this—does this mean that the lifesaver goes about his duties with a negative attitude toward the entire matter of swimming and toward the swimmers in his pool?

Should he carry on the job in a grim fashion?

Well, maybe some lifesavers do.

But, that is hardly the proper way.

Nor should the Christian Business Person sport a sour, bitter approach to the daily routine. The Christian should be realistic and realize that the business world is often going to disagree with the Bible.

WE DON'T WANT SATISFIED CUSTOMERS.

At an automobile manufacturing company sales school the instructor shocked the students with the comment, "We don't want satisfied customers." He was amused at their reaction and quickly added, "A satisfied customer never buys anything. If a person is satisfied with the car that he or she is driving, it is difficult or almost impossible to sell that person a new one.

"If a man is satisfied that he has a good wife he will not go around searching for a replacement. Your job, as sales people, is to spread dissatisfaction."

The class soon understood their mission: spread dissatisfaction. Spread dissatisfaction about the competitors product. Spread dissatisfaction about the old car the customer is presently driving. Keep spreading dissatisfaction until the potential buyer succumbs and signs on the dotted line.

Advertising is another way of planting the seeds of dissatisfaction.

Whatever happened to meeting the needs of the customer? That is certainly not the point. The point is to convince the customer that anyone who doesn't buy the product lacks good common sense. The objective is the sale of the product.

THEY'RE CHEAPSKATES, CROOKS, LIARS

One day a businessman visited his advertising agency. "Bill, I want you to write some radio copy that will convince those folks out there (pointing in every direction) that my competitors are a bunch of cheapskates, crooks, and liars. Their product is a fraud and I want everybody to know it."

Bill had many years of experience in advertising. His agency had a reputation for truthfulness in every claim that they made. His reputation as a Christian was known throughout the community.

"Calm down, I'll have no part in advertising with that objective. I know there are many advertisers who believe that the way to sell their product is to point out all the deficiencies of the competitors products.

"This agency doesn't condone that type of presentation. Why not emphasize the positive side? Let us tell your potential buyers about the excellent qualities of your product, your service, your reputation, and your interest in their total satisfaction."

A few days later Bill met again with the businessman. Within a short time the conversation got around, once more, to the important business of the day: how should the product be advertised? They wouldn't criticize the competition. They wouldn't even mention the competition. The ad man had another idea. The businessman gave in.

"O.K. You know what I need. We have X number of dollars to spend. Do the best you can with that amount of money."

The straightforward, positive approach worked.

Within a short time that client's business accounted for twenty-five percent of the agency's billing. They've developed a warm relationship. The businessman completely trusts Bill. He trusts him because he's seen the company's principles out in the open. Satisfaction—not dissatisfaction—made the difference.

Several years later Bill was considering retiring. A friend from another agency visited him.

"I understand you have given some thought to retirement. I have a good agency. If I took over your clients it would be even better. I'm willing to talk. Maybe this is just what you have been hoping would happen."

"What do you have in mind?"

"Something based on earnings. You know how much profit your agency accounts for each year. Suppose we arrive at some agreement along those lines?"

"Before we talk money," said Bill, "tell me about your agency. What type of clientele do you have? Ever since I started this agency I've been very selective about the products I advertise. For example, I will not advertise liquor."

"I have one liquor account," Ed admitted. "I see no objection to that. If I didn't write his ads someone else would. After all, business is business. Just because I advertise the stuff doesn't mean that I drink any of it."

"That's not the point, Ed. I won't advertise anything I couldn't or wouldn't buy myself. I'd hate to think that I ever encouraged anyone to start down the road to alcoholism."

"O.K. Bill, I'm willing to drop that account. It isn't a very large percentage of my business anyway. You couldn't possibly object to my other accounts. These people are my friends. I go after my friends for business."

"You and I think differently," said Bill. "I don't make clients of my friends. I make friends of my clients. My agency was founded on the principle that every single line of copy must tell the truth. We stay out of the gray areas. We have never had the Better Business Bureau on our backs for anything."

The two ad men met a second time. Bill turned down the man's offer but did it in such a way that he made a friend. He turned aside a sweet financial transaction because of his convictions.

STRETCHING THE TRUTH

There is a belief that every successful sales person is an extrovert, an optimist, and a person who stretches the truth. The first two are good habits. Exaggeration is not.

However, sales managers are prone to wink at such traits as long as the orders keep rolling in.

It would be unfair to brand every sales person as dishonest. Yet, whether deserving the reputation or not, he or she is still under a cloud of distrust. Buyers seem to be constantly on the defensive. Suspicion is part of the process. This is not a new development. It has always been more or less an accepted fact that sales people are that way. One sales person tried to reassure her client.

"I'm only trying to do you good."

To which the customer replied: "And I'm just afraid that some day you will."

This stretching the truth gets worse every year and has resulted in laws concerning honesty in advertising, truth in packaging, and labeling with controls of every sort.

The business world's answer to this has been the escape clause, phrases and clauses built into contracts to provide an interpretation that is often completely foreign to the understanding of the buyer. They are statements written to conceal an alternate meaning that is only brought to light when the terms of the contract are contested.

NICE SALE, GEORGE, BUT . . .

After writing an exceptionally large contract a sales person got a call from the company attorney.

"George, that was a nice sale you made, one of the largest the company has ever been favored with. However, we cannot accept the contract the way you have it written."

"What's wrong with it?"

"You haven't included any escape clauses in it. It binds us up too tight."

"What do you mean, escape clauses? That sounds like a lot of double-talk to me."

"No, it's not double-talk—just a sentence that can be interpreted more ways than one."

They argued the point at length, but the attorney prevailed.

Finally George said, "O.K., you write up the contract the way you want it to be, but I reserve the right to point out the loopholes to the customer. Then, if he elects to sign it, I will feel that I have done my duty to all concerned."

The customer didn't consider the few changes very serious and the deal was closed. The action, in this case, further solidified an excellent customer-salesperson relationship with this good account. Without full disclosure of the facts, the changed contract may never have been signed.

Deceitful tactics are not the hallmark of a reputable or Christian salesperson, or one who seeks to live within the bounds of good business ethics. He is travelling a different path and a difficult one. The going may be rough, but the rewards are worthwhile. A reputation for honesty assures good customer relations.

SELLING ABOVE ALL

There are occasions when the buyer seems to want to believe a lie because it fits in with her hopes or plans. She may need quick delivery and so believes the promises of impossible delivery dates made to her by unscrupulous salespeople. Many customers have been lured into deals that could often bring serious problems and bitter regrets.

Knowing that certain promises are not binding even when made in writing, it is tempting to make such promises, but it doesn't bring about good customer relations.

There is almost always competition. A business person worried that he is about to lose an order may resort to unethical practices such as planting doubts in the mind of the buyer.

Should a Christian follow these same tactics? Not unless there is some strong evidence that the buyer is making a choice that will get him into real trouble. A good salesperson might even give some warnings but is never to plant malicious doubts.

Unscrupulous salespeople are tempted to resort to bribery to obtain orders. An ethical, Christian, conscientious salesperson should never tempt a purchasing agent with gifts or kickbacks.

HOW ABOUT IT, VERN?

On one occasion a salesperson found himself violating this rule. Vern was a good customer of his. As manager of a large commissary he bought many of his supplies from this salesperson. Hardly a week went by without an order for something. It seemed to the salesperson that whenever he called to see Vern, Vern would make some remark about the good clothing he was wearing. The salesperson fell into a trap: He misunderstood these remarks to mean that Vern was trying to get the salesperson to buy him a suit.

"Vern," he said, "I'd like to have my tailor fit you up with a good suit. How about it?"

He'll never forget the look that came over Vern's face. He just stared at the salesperson for a while and then said:

"I could never do the thing that you have suggested."

The salesperson was disgusted with himself. He paid dearly for that mistake. It was a year before he got another order from Vern. He learned a bitter lesson and never tried that again.

PITFALLS AND BENEFITS

There is another pitfall that a Christian business person must avoid—downgrading your competitors' products. It may be tempting, but it's also vicious. Still, it's becoming more and more a common practice.

Should the Christian fall in line and join the pack to tear down the reputation of fellow business people? Consider this advice: "Never try to climb to success on another person's shoulders." It is far more satisfying to point out the salient features of your own product than to call attention to the defects in your competitors' products.

It could be that their products are superior. You would be dishonest to downgrade it, but you could provide better delivery, easier terms, a longer or stronger guarantee, a lower price or better service. Let the customer do the comparing. Your job is to present the facts honestly and convincingly.

Sometimes it's better to lose an order. Surely, it's much better than losing a customer.

There are benefits to not criticizing your competitors.

One very successful salesperson could be friends with his competitors because they knew he didn't criticize their products. Many were his valued friends. They often had lunch or played golf together.

On occasion they passed along valuable tips to each other concerning product lines in which they did not compete. They respected each other. The exceptions were very few, the benefits invaluable.

A business person should approach every sale with a long-range objective in view. Honesty and fair dealing should be inseparably linked with our Christian testimony.

Such behavior does not always ensure material success. Nevertheless, regardless of the outcome, there should be no compromise. This has to be the way of a dedicated Christian salesperson.

The Christian business person is also careful about personal expense accounts. Padding accounts is illegal—but also unfair to the employer.

A certain amount of entertainment is desirable. A luncheon, a dinner, concert, golf game, or fishing trip may be permissible. Such occasions help bring about a sense of comradeship. In response to such considerations, a salesperson may be invited to the home of a customer. Friendships such as this may endure for years.

It's easier to do business with your friends than with your enemies.

A deal is never completed when the product is delivered and paid for. There must be complete satisfaction on the part of the buyer that should last for the life of the material or equipment sold. Such satisfaction is certain to bring repeat orders. This is the responsibility of the Christian business person.

At one time, a person's word was as good as his bond. Some say this is no longer true. Trustworthy salespeople have proven that sometimes the best commitments are not those written by contract makers. Rather, they are often business deals based on verbal promises between friends with absolute confidence on both sides. This is Christian business at its best.

A LITTLE BIT OF POCKET MONEY

John was a pharmacist who got very excited about a new drug and sent out five hundred letters to a select group of patients, detailing the trade name and manufacturer, and mentioning that his pharmacy stocked the over-the-counter item.

He considered this a service to his customers and felt the use of the drug product, and also the benefit for the welfare of his patients, justified the cost and the time.

Several weeks later, the company salesperson came by the store, and John showed him the letter. He was elated to find this unsolicited endorsement of the new product, asked permission to take a copy to the home office, and inquired how much the printing had cost.

After several months, he returned. In the privacy of John's office he handed him cash to cover the expense.

"The company frequently pays for printing costs that spell out the name of their products."

No one witnessed the cash that was given in the transaction. The money could be pocketed without reporting it. The salesperson would bury it in his expense account. This way the company had no payments to explain.

John was that much richer—in tax-free dollars. What a temptation for a Christian.

John took the money. Bill held to his convictions. So did George. But not so the salesperson who wanted to buy Vern a suit or John, who also gave in.

You can go either way when confronted with the downward pull.

You have to be ready.

Part Two

THE PRICE
OF ETHICS

CHAPTER 4

What Can Ethics Cost?

IT CAN COST MONEY

The judge had served on the municipal court bench for a number of years. He had a sterling reputation for law enforcement. Many a traffic violator had tried to squirm out of paying a fine. Not in this judge's court. He showed no partiality.

The day came when the judge found himself on the other side of the bench. He and his wife were vacationing. As they cruised along, chatting with each other, occupied with the scenery, listening to the news on the radio, they did not observe the highway patrol following along behind them until the judge saw the red lights flashing in his rearview mirror.

There was no argument. The judge had been speeding.

Then the highway patrol officer discovered he'd apprehended a judge and closed the citation book.

Touching his cap he said, "Sorry, judge, you were going a

bit fast. Watch it. Keep it safe. You know the limit is fifty-five."

"Oh, no," said the judge. "You just go ahead and give me the ticket. I violated the law. When anyone appears in my court I don't care who he is, he gets the same treatment as anyone else. I was speeding. I deserve the fine."

The officer shrugged and wrote out the ticket, setting a date for the judge to appear before a nearby magistrate. The judge studied the situation, then turned to wife.

"We might as well go right in to see this fellow and get the matter settled."

The magistrate had the same reaction as the patrol officer.

"Sorry about this judge. I'll take care of it. You and your wife enjoy your trip, but take it easy."

Again the judge protested.

"No, I show no partiality in my court. I believe in the Golden Rule. I don't deny the charge. I'm willing to pay the fine."

The magistrate was surprised but soon recovered and "threw the book" at the judge.

A CAREER

Carl had been associated with the transportation world for over thirty years. He was concerned with the increasing erosion of moral standards.

Working for three large national transportation companies, Carl did a lot of national account calling.

Executives of these companies frequently suggested to Carl, sometimes bluntly, at other times casually: "If your company wants our business, you'll have to work with us to reduce our transportation costs."

In other words, they wanted him to "short weight" their shipments. If the trailer weighed a full 50,000 pounds, the invoice was expected to show possibly only 40,000 pounds, thus reducing the charge substantially.

East Coast garment and clothing manufacturers purposely falsified the description of their shipments to take advantage of a different and lower rate classification.

Transportation managers, purchasing agents, and others who could influence the volume of business, expected under-the-table kickbacks, either in monetary form or in added service such as lavish entertainment.

Certain transportation facilities maintained a stable of call girls in various major cities for the pleasure of their major accounts.

Shipping clerks in a number of large organizations were expected to solicit cash kickbacks to augment their earnings. This took the pressure off management to increase salaries.

The kickbacks were part of the package.

Carl couldn't go along. As a result, Carl lost promotions on several occasions.

"Carl, everyone else is doing it. Why not fall in line?"

He was effective without falling in line. He was able to obtain a good volume of business. He helped organize marketing and sales programs to show substantial profit. Finally, Carl left the transportation industry. His ethical standards cost him his job. But, at least he could live with himself.

PROMOTIONS

Jim spent his entire life fighting a losing battle against unethical practices. On his first job, his boss continually asked him to cover for him. Finally came the showdown. A certain person called on his boss. Jim knocked on the manager's office door and announced the man.

"Tell him I'm out," the manager barked. Jim stood in the doorway somewhat amazed. He couldn't lie. When the manager noticed Jim hadn't done what he was told he shouted,

"Go at once and tell him I'm out."

Timorously, Jim answered, "I'm sorry, sir, I just can't do that."

"You can't do that? Damn you! You'll do exactly as I tell you. Otherwise take your hat and go home."

So Jim went home. It was just lunch time. All the way home Jim wondered how he could break the news to his mother. But he said nothing during the lunch until his mother said, "Jim, hurry up now. Finish your lunch, and go right back to work, or you'll be late."

"Mother . . . I'm sacked," said Jim.

His mother sat down with a puzzled look on her face. "What have you been doing, Jim, that caused that?"

The whole story came out. Jim's mother listened and then said,

"You hurry up now. Finish your lunch, and go right back to work. I'll be praying for you."

"But, Mother, don't you understand? I don't have a job!"

"Yes, I know," she answered. "Remember the verse you learned: 'Them that honor Me, I will honor'? Now I'm going to pray. You put on your hat and off you go."

Greatly wondering, Jim did just that, and took his place as usual behind the counter. Shortly thereafter the manager came in. Casting a sidelong glance at Jim, he made no comment and went to his office.

At the end of the week, the manager sent for Jim, who was

sure it was all over now. Imagine his surprise when the manager said:

"Jim, I've an apology to make. You're a better man than I am. I've given instructions to the bookkeeper to increase your wages."

His ethics had served him well. Years later, Jim joined a firm of road transport operators with headquarters in Ireland. The firm had high principles, so much so that they had even taken out a bond worth £30,000 as a promise that their vehicles would not be used to transport goods liable to duty across the border. This rule was very strictly enforced.

Not long after Jim joined the firm, he was asked to arrange transportation for some cartons containing empty chocolate boxes to be used for a display at an exhibition he was giving in the Dublin area. The boxes would be loaded in Belfast. Since they were empties, they would not be subject to duty. This is how Jim arranged the consignment.

Imagine his surprise and alarm when he received a call saying three buses had been impounded by Customs. All the passengers were stranded at the border. There was a threat that the bond would be called. Jim was being blamed.

Customs had opened one of the large cartons and found below a layer of empty boxes many rows of complete boxes of chocolates, which were, of course, a highly dutiable article. Jim's job was in jeopardy. He and a friend took a walk on a beach outside Dublin. Sinking down on their knees, they committed the whole matter to the Lord.

Jim kept his job. Some time later he learned that when the matter had been broached at board level, it was his reputation as an ethical man that had saved him.

Eventually, the firm merged with four similar companies.

As in all such mergers, jealousies arose among the staff members, all of whom were seeking the best positions. Rivalry was the order of the day. Jim became a casualty. Caught in a deceitful plot by a rival, Jim was demoted and transferred at a considerable loss of salary.

Eventually Jim moved to Durban, South Africa, to become General Manager of Transport. There, as a result of his desire to serve the Lord, he became involved in the arrangements for a Billy Graham evangelical rally.

On the night before the rally, the internationally known Indian Market was burned out. News of the tragedy got through to Dr. Graham at his hotel. He immediately went down to the market to bring what consolation he could to the Indians who had suffered such a severe loss.

He prayed with them and assured them that on his return to the United States, he would put their need before his organization, and would send them some monetary relief.

On the day of the rally, the mayor of the city attended. Jim was responsible for the offering. He made it clear that the offering taken that afternoon would be used to defray the expenses of the rally, which were considerable. No mention whatever was made of the promise that Dr. Graham had given to the Indian Market owners.

The following morning, a banner headline in the local press read:

MAYOR SAYS "GRAHAM PRAYS, BUT TAKES THE MONEY." A story had been released to the press that those who gave at the rally had been under the impression that any surplus would be given to the market. This was in fact never stated, or even implied. Much harm was done. Jim was at the center of the controversy.

The following year, while on business in Atlantic City, Jim was approached by the press officer of the Billy Graham organization, who produced a Canadian newspaper that had been released that day, carrying an article allegedly written by a Canadian correspondent who had been in Durban, repeating the accusation that while Dr. Graham had prayed for the Indians, he had failed to pass over the money collected.

Jim wrote a letter in reply, setting out the facts, but found that he had made a real enemy in the mayor.

"How," the mayor asked, "could he have gotten to the market before I did, and why didn't he keep his promise to send money to help?"

In fact, Dr. Graham had done exactly as he had promised to do. He had raised the matter with his organization on his return to headquarters and a very generous donation had been sent. This act, however, had received no publicity in the local press.

Jim learned that sometimes sticking with your ethics can detour a career and even cut away at social position.

A CANCELLED ORDER

Two travellers checked into a hotel in the late afternoon. They were strangers to each other but, as travellers do, they soon got into conversation with each other. The younger of the two represented one of the federal banks for cooperatives. Paul was a sales engineer for a dairy equipment manufacturer.

"What brings you to this town?" the younger man inquired.

"Well, you see, I sold some equipment to a large dairy company. They have a small processing plant in this town and they are improving it with modern machinery. I'm here to look over the project and plan for the installation crew. What is your business?"

"I'm a banker," the young man replied. "A group of dairy farmers in this area contacted us. They would like to start a farmer's cooperative creamery. I'm here in response to their inquiry. They are looking for us to finance the project."

"A dairy co-op?" Paul couldn't believe it. "Why, there aren't enough cows in the whole county to supply the milk for one plant. Surely not enough milk to warrant the construction of another processing unit. That would be foolish."

The men talked at length about the merits of financing the construction of another plant in the area. Perhaps the best thing to do would be for the large dairy to sell their processing unit to the farmers rather than have two plants in the town, neither of which would be able to earn sufficient funds to pay for its upkeep. The young banker agreed and suggested that he would present the matter to the dairy farmers at his scheduled meeting with them the next morning.

Paul had to make a decision. Should he meet with the farmers and get in on the ground floor for the sale of a lot of machinery they would need in the construction of a dairy processing unit? Or should he warn the customers of the dangers of the plan?

Warning them of the dangers was obviously the best thing, but it would mean the customer would cancel the equipment order if they elected to sell the processing plant.

The company would frown on that. Paul would lose a sizeable commission on the deal. Perhaps the easiest thing to do would be to go ahead and deliver the equipment. After all, it wasn't his problem.

This kind of reasoning didn't fit in with his Christian standards for doing business, however.

The best course was to allow the customers to be the judge in the matter and accept their decision regardless of the consequences. He informed his associates in the company and they agreed.

The next morning he called on the general manager of the large dairy and told him the whole story. Then he suggested that inasmuch as the farmers were determined to go ahead with their plans, it would be wise for the dairy to sell them the processing plant. He recommended that they follow his advice. The general manager responded as Paul thought he would.

"That sounds like a sensible idea and the right move to make. In that case we would not need all the machinery that we have on order with you. Would your company be willing to accept a cancellation?"

"I've thought about that," Paul replied. "I have already discussed that with our people. We're willing to accept the cancellation of your order without penalty. Naturally, we don't like cancellations but we believe this is the best procedure for all concerned."

The farmers bought the processing plant, as it enabled them to start their own enterprise at once and gave them complete control of the market area.

However, Paul ultimately got his sale. The farmers purchased the equipment that had been cancelled. Paul gained new respect with the large dairy, too. Their confidence in Paul and his company increased and became a permanent thing.

DID THEY REALLY LOSE?

Did the four individuals really lose? The judge paid a fine he could have sidestepped. But, he had greater respect for himself and received increased respect from others.

Jim lost promotions but kept his internal peace. He survived as well. Today he has a good job.

Carl had to switch careers but is excited and happy, and finds his new work a challenge.

Paul lost a sale—but only temporarily. He gained business in the long run.

No one who sticks by his ethical principles really loses.

CHAPTER 5

Good Ethics
Can Make You Rich

BOB, THE BANKER

Bankers have a reputation, whether deserved or not, for having ice water flowing through their veins. Bob isn't that kind of a banker. His clients, as well as his employees, think he is just tops.

Bob's father taught him to walk in right paths and expected great things from him. His parents watched him step from college straight into a lucrative business opportunity. He steadily moved up the ladder of business success.

Suddenly, near tragedy struck and temporarily arrested Bob's progress. He found himself burning with fever and an almost crippling infection. Long hours of enforced rest and reflection in the healing rays of Florida sunshine restored him to good health.

During that time, at the home of his parents, Bob became a

Christian. He agreed with God to put his full trust and confidence in Jesus Christ.

Soon Bob accepted a position with one of the largest banks in the country and was placed in charge of the consumer credit department. The bank president and one of the members of the board immediately took him aside.

"Bob, when you became an officer in this bank we knew that you were a religious fanatic. Now the time has come for you to leave the church outside. We are responsible to our patrons for the millions of dollars they have deposited with us. I am a churchgoer myself," continued the bank president, "but I leave it there."

He then began to paint a beautiful picture of bonuses, changes in title, and increased income if Bob would just become one of the boys, join in the liquor parties and card games, and arrange "proper" entertainment for visiting bankers from out of town.

Bob replied, "Mr. President, the Lord Jesus Christ means more to me than everything you have talked about."

All of a sudden the bank president remembered he had an appointment. He turned over the interview to a board member who was also embarrassed and who dropped the subject.

Bob was in a tight spot and knew it. He promptly called on some of his friends in the local Christian Business Men's Committee to join with him in fervent prayer that the stand he had taken would not imperil his job.

The following Monday morning, the president greeted Bob with a big smile and slapped him on the back as if they were longtime buddies.

For a year, everything was "peaches and cream." Then the pressure began. First came ridicule, then sarcastic remarks.

Still, Bob's department, staffed with more and more born-again Christians, showed a profit that exceeded all the other departments of the bank. Finally, the bank changed presidents. Bob stayed on.

The transition was smooth. The new president wrote Bob a memo:

"You are on your own. Hire the help you feel are most effective. You are welcome to come into my office any time."

Taking advantage of this offer Bob often witnessed to his chief concerning the transforming power of a full commitment to Jesus Christ.

The consumer credit department, under Bob's full control, soon accounted for fifty-one percent of the bank's total earnings after taxes. The bank examiner complimented the bank president on the operation, which was cleaner than any bank in that section of the country. Charge-offs of bad accounts were less than one-fourth of one percent, while other banks had charge-offs totalling as much as three percent against reserves. While examining other banks, examiners often phoned Bob to ask if certain things were right or correct. He was allowed to run his own trials and check these controls with the examiner in charge. The new president doubled Bob's salary. His staff of mainly born-again Christians increased to thirty by this time. The bank added three more floors to take care of the increased business.

A merger with another bank brought nineteen branch banks under Bob's control. The consolidation brought a new president who called Bob to appear before the directors to congratulate him on the most profitable operation in the bank. After all the compliments and eulogy, Bob thanked the board members and then gave three reasons for his excellent results:

1. Divine help.
2. A dedicated staff that undertook to accomplish a more satisfactory job than the average employee.
3. Hard work.

A number of the branch managers were present at the meeting. Later in the day some of them called on Bob to congratulate him and tell him how he had challenged them to stand up for their convictions.

The new president liked Bob's management but was uneasy with his stringent standards. He tried unsuccessfully to get Bob into the party circuit. Frustrated, he applied some real pressure, withholding any increase in Bob's salary until such a time as Bob would go along. The siege lasted for eight long years, during which Bob claimed the promise of Isaiah 54:17:

"No weapon that is formed against thee shall prosper; and every tongue that shall rise against thee in judgment thou shalt condemn. This is the heritage of the servants of the Lord, and their righteousness is of me, saith the Lord."

Finally, a questionable transaction forced the president to resign to save face. A fourth president moved in and took over. One of his first official activities was to call Bob into his office for a meeting.

"Bob, I notice by the records before me that you are the only senior executive in this bank who has not had a salary change for eight years. What should we do about it?"

"Well, Mr. President, living costs during that period of time have risen some 34½ percent. My department has continued to turn in over a million dollars in profits each year, so use your own judgment." He did.

Bob's salary was increased 35 percent with a compensating increase in the amount of his pension at retirement.

Pressure continued in another form. The personnel manager

tried to have a rule change made that would require Bob to requisition all new help through him. He hoped to stop Bob's tendency to hire Christians.

It didn't work. Other department heads in the bank phoned Bob when they needed tellers, secretaries, or other help. They were impressed with the type of employee he hired. God sent him top quality employees from all over the United States.

Bob's story proved over and over again that God is faithful to those who refuse to move away from honest dealing and good ethical business practices.

A BOOKSELLER'S PROBLEMS

A publisher and retailer of books must have an uncanny ability to select books the public will buy. How can they determine ahead of time which book will turn out to be a best seller?

The retailer also has other problems. Certainly a religious bookstore cannot and will not stock or sell pornographic books. This is an obvious and easy decision to make. The lines, in such a case, are sharply drawn.

At other times, though, the decision to sell or not to sell a certain book becomes very difficult.

Bill and his wife faced all these questions when they started in business. They decided to open a religious bookstore in a college town and rented a small place with just about 1000 square feet of area.

Their pleasing personalities, plus a good knowledge of the religious book business, enabled them to grow to a point where they were forced to expand. They moved into a store four times the size of their original store, with a corresponding increase in rent.

The enlarged area enabled them to display their merchandise better, bringing increased sales, but not enough to match increased costs. They had to find some additional lines of merchandise or books to help boost sales. The need for greater sales volume was urgent.

An enterprising salesperson for a very questionable publishing house sensed that Bill and his wife needed an expanded inventory to augment their sales. He had been anxious to secure an outlet for his company in this city, but Bill had always turned down his publications.

The salesperson knew Bill needed to increase his sales volume in a hurry. The line of merchandise he had to offer would easily double Bill's total sales. Across a luncheon table he dangled perhaps the biggest "plum" Bill had ever been offered. His efforts were all in vain.

"No," said Bill, "I need sales and I need them badly but I'll never stock your line of books."

"Look, Bill," he replied, "I'll have a line of customers outside your door every Monday morning waiting for you to open up so they can buy my books. You'll have more business than you can handle."

Again the answer was negative. The salesperson tried hard to convince Bill. He tempted him with large profits and many other inducements, but to no avail. Bill stood firm with his convictions.

Bill and his wife now have three bookstores, all staffed with devoted employees. Their customers have full confidence that everything offered for sale in their stores is sound reading. Such a firm stand is often difficult to explain to the banker when you need a loan. Still, Bill's line of credit at the bank is excellent.

Bill's success is directly traceable to his stand on ethics.

EARL CAN GET IT WHOLESALE

The wholesale grocery business has always been a low profit enterprise. Seldom, if ever, do the profits reach double-digit percentages. To offset some of the low margin items that must be carried in stock, most wholesalers carry a few items with better profit percentages, even though they are hardly groceries.

Earl was president and owner of a chain of wholesale and retail grocery stores and also a devout Christian. In addition, he was president of a very large bank.

Each year Earl travelled to various parts of the country to purchase such items as canned fruit, vegetables, and fish. On these trips he sought out Christian business people for fellowship as well as for good tips on market conditions throughout the nation. One day, one of these friends challenged Earl: "Is it right for a Christian to engage in the sale of alcoholic beverages, cigarettes, questionable books? All are high profit items but represent some of the biggest challenges to physical, emotional, and spiritual health in our country."

As Earl journeyed homeward after this luncheon he had a lot of time to ponder the problem of questionable sales from his outlets. He prayed about it. By the time he reached his home, he had decided cigarettes and liquor had to go. He would no longer offer these items for sale in his stores. He called his manager in to his office.

"We're discontinuing the sale of liquor and cigarettes as of today. Return every case and carton to our suppliers as fast as you can." His manager looked at him in dismay.

"Earl, you must be out of your mind. Those items account for a whopping big percentage of our profits. Not only that—if you take such items off the shelves, you will drive out the customers. They will go to our competitors to pick up those items and you will lose their grocery business as well."

"I've thought that all through. The business is mine and I can do as I please. If we end up the year in the red, I'll take the blame."

The merchandise in question was returned to the suppliers but not without a lot of argument. Many of them did their best to get Earl to change his mind but to no avail. Earl's decision was made in full trust that God would honor the action. To Earl there was no retreat from his position.

When the reason for this bold move became known, more customers than ever patronized Earl's stores.

Increased profits were the result. Earl's stand was vindicated.

THE MEDICINE MAN

Ralph faced a similar problem. He was a pharmacist just out of college with a diploma and a license to compound drugs and dispense them. But he wanted nothing to do with what he thought were the most dangerous drugs—cigarettes and alcohol—and he discreetly said this to his boss in the drugstore.

However, Ralph soon discovered irregularities in the prescription department that he couldn't condone. His protests were too much for the boss though and Ralph was dismissed after only three months.

He wasn't discouraged. He soon had a better job that wouldn't have been offered if he hadn't been available at the time. One thing bothered him about the new job. He had to work on Sundays, which he felt was a day of worship dedicted to the Lord. He vowed, "If ever I have a pharmacy of my own it won't be open on Sunday, regardless of what other drugstores do."

That day came. Ralph opened up his first business venture, an exclusive prescription drugstore in a neighborhood close to the hospital where he had been employed for ten years as a pharmacist. Advisors doubted it would be a success. Not enough doctors in the vicinity, they said.

Bad location, they said, as it was directly across the street from a drugstore that had been in business in the same location for ten years or more. Silly to be closed on Sunday. Customers would surely patronize the competitor whose shop was open seven days a week.

But it didn't turn out that way. From the very first day enough business came in. Within six months Ralph had to hire another pharmacist.

More doctors moved into the area. Within the short space of two or three years, there were several doctors' office buildings completed or in progress. Ralph's business grew rapidly. Two more pharmacists were hired. Three other drugstores moved into the area. Ralph's business increased all the more. Ralph provided just the kind of service the doctors and patients liked. Better service. Quicker handling of the prescriptions. An exclusive pharmacy could do more. Ralph proved it. A favorite verse of Ralph's is found in Proverbs 3:5,6:

"Trust in the Lord with all thine heart: and lean not unto thine own understanding. In all thy ways acknowledge him and He shall direct thy paths."

After fifteen years in the first location near the hospital, a freeway was built through the city just a block away from the store. A large medical facility was torn down, forcing many of the doctors to move out of the area. Ralph moved to a new building where two doctors had offices, only to discover the building was not zoned for a pharmacy. Ralph needed a variance from the city planning commission. This he got. Then, a competitive pharmacist appealed the variance by going directly to the city council and urging them to negate the commission's decision. The council voted—a four-to-four tie, which automatically upheld the ruling of the planning commission. The competition filed another appeal, because one of the council members had been absent when the vote was taken. This time, the vote was five to four in favor of Ralph's request. It was a time of rejoicing in the Lord's promise that "no good thing will He withhold from those who walk uprightly." (Psalm 84:11)

Ralph credits his entire success to God—and to his own adherence to biblical ethics.

HAROLD'S IN THE CONSTRUCTION BUSINESS

Harold's career in the construction business was a big success. He built houses, factories, stores, office buildings, churches, schools, hospitals, government buildings, an airport terminal, shopping centers, and many apartment buildings.

"When I started, I vowed to approach every customer, supplier, and employee with full honesty.

"I didn't make promises I couldn't keep—as far as deadlines were concerned. Sometimes I lost jobs because of it, but I gained more because of it. People would say to me:

" 'I'll go with you even though it will cost more, because I know I can believe what you say' or 'I'll go with you even though it will take longer, because I know you'll keep that promise.'

"I've established a formula. I do the best possible job I can. I work as hard as I can. Then I leave it up to God.

"Time after time, I've seen the unusual happen. I've seen Him completely change the minds of men. I've seen Him arrange a whole set of circumstances. I've seen Him get us unusually good jobs and keep us from bad ones. I've seen Him solve seemingly impossible labor problems. I've seen Him do nothing . . . to teach me a lesson.

"Many years ago we were building a small addition to a hospital. In midstream, when additional plans for a $2 million addition were submitted, we bid, but were second bidders, by just about $6000.

"We were disappointed, along with government and hospital people. They wanted to deal with the same contractor, if possible, and so wanted us to get the job. They all tried to pull strings to get us the job. But in the end they failed. The job went to the low bidder, which is as it should be.

"Several months later we learned that the contractor who got the job had been swindled out of about $200,000 by an ingenious scheme of a subcontractor who filed bankruptcy and went to South America with the money.

"Had we been the contractor on that job, it would have happened to us, as we would have used the same company.

"I remember praying, when we didn't get the job: 'Lord, what's wrong here? We're already on the job. We could use this job. It's a natural.'

"One year later, I simply prayed: 'Thank you, Lord.'

"Several years ago, we arranged to obtain a piece of land where we would build a good-sized vertical shopping center and apartment complex downtown.

"The city came up with a requirement that more land would be necessary for parking. The only land was next door, and it was occupied with buildings. I went to see the owner, and he couldn't have been less receptive. I went back with a better offer. He said it was not the money. He simply wouldn't consider it.

"I remember praying, 'Well, Lord, it looks like you don't want to be a partner in this nice new project.' I had almost forgotten the project when a friend called:

" 'I think you can go make your deal.'

"The landowner was now as nice and friendly as could be. We made the deal, and all has been fine since. No one will say why he changed his mind. But I think I know. It was just another case of leaving everything to the Lord to work out.

"Skeptics would say that in any business over a thirty-year period, there are bound to be lucky breaks that come along to make a business successful.

"True, but I've had far too many for the average business. I sincerely believe all of it has come directly from the hand of God.

"My whole life revolves around this relationship. For Jesus said, 'What shall it profit a man, if he shall gain the whole world, and lose his own soul?' " (Mark 8:36)

Harold believes that biblical ethics can make you rich. It worked in his case.

CHAPTER 6

The Bonus of a Clean Conscience

FEELING SQUEAKY CLEAN INSIDE

"Let your conscience be your guide." Such a standard allows a lot of latitude for our actions. One person's conscience may be tender and sensitive, while another's may be hardened.

The conscience of every Christian should be sensitive to the degree that it would be in control of that person's behavior.

Conscience should have the sensitivity to discern between right and wrong. This sort of conscience is a God-given quality.

Once developed, this sort of conscience can be a correct guide. Listening to that conscience, regardless of the consequences, allows a person to have a clean feeling inside. This very feeling is what nearly every troubled business person is looking for today. Some people call it peace. Some call it freedom from guilt. Others call it happiness.

On life's commodity board, nothing is more desired than

that feeling—the feeling of being completely clean inside.

You might pay the price. Loss of respect. Loss of a job. Loss of security. Whatever.

But the price is cheap for that special feeling.

Nothing beats feeling clean inside.

JERRY . . . OUT OF A JOB

Jerry had been married about two years and had a little girl about six months old. He was out of work but had a clean conscience. All because of a decision he had made at his job.

The last job he had was a good one. He liked his boss. His work was efficient.

The factory where he worked produced sweat shirts and T-shirts with various designs on the front and back, put there by a silk screen process. Jerry's job was to apply the design to the shirt—a Mickey Mouse, a Donald Duck, an American flag, or what have you.

One day his boss gave Jerry a group of silk screens, together with an order for several thousand sweat shirts. The pictures to be put on the shirts were definitely pornographic and the captions were obscene. Jerry handed the job back to his boss.

"I just couldn't do these. I'm a Christian and wouldn't want to corrupt the minds of kids with stuff like that."

"Listen, Jerry, we're getting a good price for this job and I want you to do it. Forget all that nonsense about corrupting kids' minds. They're corrupt anyway from watching TV. This is tame compared to some of the things they see."

"No, my mind is made up. I can't do that sort of work."

"If that is your decision, you better go out and get yourself another job."

Jerry left that job with a clean feeling that he had obeyed his conscience regardless of the cost.

ERNEST HAD THIS BELIEF

Ernest was the manager of a large department store in southern California. Early one October day the vice-president gave out the following directive:

> Commencing the first Sunday in November all stores are to remain open each Sunday until further notice. The hours will conform to the requirements of the shopping center in which you are located. Please arrange with your employees to take turns so that no employee will be required to work every Sunday.

Ernest was troubled. He had a conviction against working on Sunday. He could never agree to manage a store that kept open on the Lord's day.

He thought the matter through carefully. He consulted with his wife and family. Everyone agreed, so he sent his resignation to company headquarters, electing to terminate the day before the directive was to go into effect.

When Ernest's resignation reached the regional office, the vice-president was deeply moved. He too was very religious, but he didn't have the conviction Ernest did. He picked up the phone.

"Hello, Ernest, I got your letter of resignation this morning and agree with you 100 percent, but you know how competition is these days. We just have to conform. We must make this move but can't afford to lose men like you. How about reconsidering?"

"No, I've made up my mind. I can get another job. I'm still

a young fellow and not exactly broke. Don't worry about me."

"I'm not worried about you. I'm worried about the company. Men with your experience and capabilities are hard to come by. We need you in our organization.

"I'm going to make you an offer. Would you be willing to move to Pennsylvania and take a store there? Our stores back there aren't open on Sundays."

Ernest agreed. He wanted to stay with the company. He moved his family to Pennsylvania and was able to live with his conscience after that.

SENATOR HENRY

Henry was a state senator. He was also a churchgoing man with a real spiritual purpose. His goal was to serve his district according to the principles laid down in the Word of God.

He was a very outspoken man. There was never any question as to where he stood. He won his office handily. People trusted him and knew him to be a fighter.

His fellow senators trusted him. They knew that if Henry promised to vote for their bill he would do as he had promised. If he didn't like the bill that was submitted for a vote, he was equally adamant in his stand against it. This caused him trouble occasionally.

One day a bill was submitted that Henry opposed on an ethical basis. The sponsor came to him.

"Henry, are you going to vote for my bill?"

"No, I'm not. It has no credibility. It is a waste of the taxpayers' money. It's just another way for you and your henchmen to dip into the state's funds. I've read your bill carefully and can't find one good thing in it."

"Listen, Henry, think it over. I've voted for your legislation lots of times. I've given you my support and I want yours. You have a lot of influence on the floor. If you oppose my bill it may not pass. I need your support."

"You'll not get it. Not for that bill."

A few days later they met in the hall of the capitol building.

"Henry, have you changed your mind? How about giving me your vote on that bill?"

"No way. I told you that I wouldn't vote for your bill and I meant what I said."

Henry's colleague gave up on any further argument. He decided on a different course.

That weekend, when Henry went to check out of the hotel, he found his bill had been paid.

"Who paid it?"

"I really don't know, Senator. It was a lady. I had never seen her before. She paid it with cash, too. Just said that she was told to pay your bill."

The same thing happened when Henry went to settle with the garage man, the laundry man, and other regular stops. He knew what was happening.

The following Monday Henry confronted his colleague, who had a big grin on his face,

"Hello, Henry, changed your mind yet?"

"No, you know I won't."

"Listen, Henry, who do you think paid all your bills last week? There's more where that came from. You better wise up."

He stopped because he saw the determination building in Henry's face. Looking down he saw his clenched fists. The atmosphere was tense for a few moments. With one last look of consternation, Henry turned and walked away.

The battle was launched. Every bill that Henry presented

after that was voted down. Even a bill for an obviously necessary bridge across a river in his district.

"Play ball, Henry," advised his friends, "or your days here are numbered."

Henry refused—and lost the following election. To this day, he has never regretted his stand.

ETHICS FOR THE LAWYER

Ted is a lawyer and says, "There are many ways lawyers can be crooked. They can charge fees that are excessive. They can deliberately stir a simple matter into something complicated with a view to earning more and bigger fees. They can engage in that which is strictly legal but morally dishonest.

"They can join their client in dishonesty by identifying themselves with such when they know it is wrong. They simply use the magic words, 'My instructions are . . .'

"They can misrepresent their case to some third party in a way that will obtain pecuniary advantage for their client, which is theft.

"They can browbeat weaker individuals by improper use of professional expertise. They can belligerently cross-examine a witness with a view to breaking him, rather than to extracting the truth.

"No lawyer has to do that—especially a Christian. All he has to do is remain loyal to his prior commitment to Jesus Christ, which is as relevant to his practice as it is to his domestic life and his church fellowship.

"If I am asked, directly or indirectly, to misrepresent the facts, either to a court of law or to any professional business, I tell the client very plainly that I won't do it. It is not professionally ethical. Nor is it consistent with my daily practice as a dedicated Christian.

"If a client suggests impropriety, I very politely tell that person that I will not be a party to such a thing. If a client persists, I respectfully ask him to take his business elsewhere.

"Remarkably, I haven't lost a single client because of this stand. Even the most crooked prefer to trust someone whose word is their bond and will not stoop to doubtful dealing.

"How can a lawyer go into court to get a guilty person off? I won't do it. There may be many cases where there is some doubt. If I am satisfied that the person concerned is telling the truth, then I will put his case. If I detect any possible untruths, I lose confidence in my client. They may go elsewhere. Again, let me say I can't remember a single case over my whole experience where I have lost a client as a result of my stand.

"In every case, I advise 'Honesty is the best policy.' Some years ago, an accused person thanked me profusely on leaving the court; 'You saved me from prison.'

"I didn't save you from prison. You did that yourself by agreeing to tell the truth."

FOUR PRINCIPLES

A Christian lawyer will succeed in his professional practice if he is totally dedicated as a Christian to the cause of Christ first. There are four principles for a successful lawyer.

First, the person must inspire confidence so his client is not afraid to approach him and be at ease, and be continually honest.

Second, his charges must be reasonable. He should explain to his client honestly how his fees are calculated.

Thirdly, he must be prompt.

Fourthly, he must be ethical in all dealings.

"I have found in a practice that has grown from a staff of just eight to over forty in twenty-five years, that to put God first in one's professional life and to endeavour to reach other professional and business people through one's day-to-day contact with them is the way to have fulfillment.

"How can the Christian professional and business person prove the validity of the New Testament? By his life. His ethics are at the very center of this."

They give Ted that clean feeling inside.

You must have noticed from Ted's story that he not only had a clean conscience—he also had consistent success in most instances. Let's look at three more examples.

A SALES PERSON—AN AUDITOR—A SECRETARY

A very successful salesman for a large drug company informed management that he wanted to spend every weekend at home. He taught a large Bible class and his desire was to spend the Lord's day with the Lord's people.

The company honored his request and made it possible for him to arrange his travelling so that he would not be away from his church on Sundays.

The city auditor in a large city of almost half a million people worked his way up through the ranks of the accounting department. It did not take long to inform his associates that he was a Christian and would not be involved in any unethical methods of accounting.

Now, after forty years with the city, he recalls with pride

that he was never called upon at any time to falsify any reports or to condone any misuse of funds from the city treasury.

A secretary for a large high school gave testimony to the fact that she was a Christian. During the many years she held that position she had the respect of every person on the staff.

She was also proud of the fact that she never had to tell lies or make any false statements at the request of her superiors.

Part Three

WHERE DOES
THE BUCK STOP?

CHAPTER 7

The Responsibility
of Saying No

THE HITLER MENTALITY

The war crimes trials that followed World War II spawned a genuine controversy. Many of the German leaders on trial argued that they did what they did only because "we were under orders."

The judges didn't accept this. Neither did the public, which chimed in: "Sometimes you have to say no."

You might even say, "Certainly I couldn't have pushed the buttons or turned the switches to exterminate all those Jewish people in the concentration camps."

Unfortunately, that isn't true, as was proven by a unique experiment.

The experiment involved a series of word association tests supposedly to see what effect the threat of pain has on learning.

The supervisor of the test explained the procedure to the two participants.

"Subject A will be asked to make the word associations from memory.

"Subject B will administer an electric shock to subject A every time he makes the wrong choice.

"Each error will bring a greater electrical shock than the previous error. If subject A gets the association correct there will be no electrical shock.

"We will learn from the experiment whether subject A can concentrate better under the threat of pain."

Then the word associations began.

Of course, none of it was true. Subject A wasn't being tested at all. He was a part of the experiment. Nor was any electric charge being transmitted. However, subject A was pretending to feel every shock. The first mistake brought just a small sting. No problem. Then definite pain. Each shock was taken more seriously by subject A. Eventually, he was pleading with subject B to stop.

The person administering the shocks didn't know it was a fake. As far as he was concerned, the jolts were getting stronger and stronger each time, the pain greater and greater, the protests louder and more hysterical.

The study was on subject B. The question to be resolved was: How far would he go? Would he keep on shocking subject A out of loyalty to a single college experiment? Would he continue until the person lapsed into unconsciousness? (Fake, but real as far as subject B was concerned.)

The findings were startling. An incredible number of the persons pressing the botton actually went past the point where they would have killed the other subject if the shocks had been real.

Most Americans would have found themselves on trial at

Nuremberg if they had been German military leaders in World War II. We could have killed millions of Jewish people as easily as did the Germans.

We are capable of the ultimate act of "passing the buck."

We must let God develop our consciences so we will know when to say no.

JACK WOULDN'T

Jack is a man who can say no. He is a Christian attorney working in the office of a large corporation. He often finds himself in a tight spot with executives asking him to write favorable instead of unfavorable reports. One day a vice-president asked him to expand health liability payment reports to give the company a better break with IRS. Jack didn't want to state over his signature that these contingent liabilities were more specific and definite than they actually were. Yet, Jack knew the vice-president felt very strongly about the matter. It was important to the company that they get the benefit of every lawful deduction.

To the vice-president's surprise and dismay, Jack refused to sign the memo as requested. The vice-president became very angry with Jack and, as a consequence, Jack lost some of his superior officer's goodwill. In good conscience though Jack could not have acted otherwise.

Recently, one of the company's marketing managers came up with some promotional ideas that Jack considered improper under the federal laws. After the promotional plan had been explained to him, Jack countered in a kindly but firm way that the program would not satisfy federal requirements. He tried to avoid sounding as if he were sermonizing, but his remarks were greeted with an angry blast from the marketing manager, who proceeded to criticize Jack loudly for having taken such a position.

On other occasions Jack has said no to the president and others concerning improper practices. How does Jack know when to say no?

"I sense a need to be ever vigilant so my Christian principles do not become eroded by the many factual variables. I use the Bible, including the Ten Commandments and Christ's teachings, as Amos did the plumb line, to measure true honesty and morality. It's a full-time challenge and responsibility."

AN ADMIRAL TAKES A STAND

The operation of the army, navy, air force, marines, or Coast Guard is, in essence, the same as the operation of any big business enterprise.

The men in charge are committed to do the best possible job at the lowest possible cost with the facilities at hand.

The code of ethics should be just as exacting in the military establishment as it is in any corporate enterprise. And the advent of war should not abrogate that code of ethics. Some may think that anything goes in time of war, but historians are not lax in pointing out breaches of justice or compromise with what is right. War should not be an excuse for a breakdown in morals or a relaxation in a rigid code of ethics.

Frank was an admiral with thirty-eight years of service in the armed forces. He started out as a cadet in one of the United States military academies and rose to the rank of rear admiral, upper half.

He became a Christian just before his teen years—then just

drifted without much Christian growth, primarily because he neglected regular communication with God through prayer and the reading of the Bible.

As Frank moved up the ladder of success, however, he came to realize what Christ meant to him as his Lord and Savior. He did nothing to climb that ladder at the expense of others, and he knew that whatever success he had had was due to the Lord's guidance and love. His Lord never forsook him despite his neglect of Him.

During the crucial part of World War II, the Nazi wolfpacks of submarines almost brought the Allies to their knees. These subs sank millions of tons of shipping in the Atlantic.

The top military command had to develop a policy to conserve what few elements we had to combat these submarine units or wolfpacks.

An order was issued by the military high command not to stop or become dead in the water in order to pick up Germans or others who happened to be floating in the water as a result of our actions.

A ship, dead in the water, engaged in picking up men, was a sitting duck and could itself be easily picked off by any lurking enemy submarine.

As the commanding officer of a division of destroyer escorts assigned specifically to hunting down enemy submarines, Frank had to decide what action he, as a Christian, would take under these conditions.

This was no easy decision to make.

After much prayer and thought regarding the problem he decided his ships would pick up any live survivors they saw floating in the ocean.

This decision made the men in his division feel good. They knew they would be picked up if ever they found themselves in the same circumstances.

Had Frank lost a unit, even one man, or endangered operations by not adhering to the task force policy, he would have been relieved of his command and properly disciplined.

But he felt he had to say no. The Lord honored Frank's trust. The admiral never lost a ship or a man. The morale of his division was exceedingly high. By all standards they excelled in all phases of their operation. The Lord honors those who trust in Him completely—those who know when to say no.

CHAPTER 8

Bankruptcy:
The Easy Way Out

A RASH OF BANKRUPTCIES

In recent years, the United States Office of Education has lost more than $20 million in loans as thousands of ex-students have declared bankruptcy. The number of recent defaults was more than had occurred in the entire previous fifteen years of state and federal educational loan programs.

Students need not file for bankruptcy simply because they are unable at the time to repay their loans. The government makes it easy for anyone to file a petition in bankruptcy under what is known as Chapter Eleven of the bankruptcy law.

This law permits the borrower to take as much extra time as the court may allow for the repayment of the loan.

Consider the following excerpts from Chapter Eleven:

> The filing of a petition in bankruptcy is in effect a caveat, giving notice to the whole world, and is in effect an attachment

and injunction restraining all persons from interfering with property and assets of the bankrupt, the bankruptcy court being regarded as having custody and control of the bankrupt property.—Section 721, Note 3

Where no receiver or trustee is appointed, the debtor shall continue in possession of his property and shall have all the title and exercise all the powers of a trustee appointed under the title, subject, however, at all times to the control of the court and to such limitations, restrictions, terms and conditions as the court may from time to time prescribe.—Section 742

The receiver or trustee, or the debtor in possession, shall have the power upon authorization by and subject to the control of the court, to operate the business and manage the property of the debtor during such a period as the court may from time to time fix, and during such operation or management shall file reports thereof with the court at such intervals as the court may designate.—Section 743

The confirmation of an arrangement shall discharge a debtor from all his unsecured debts and liabilities provided for by the arrangement, except as provided in the arrangement.—Section 771

TWO STUDENTS

Tom and Florence were brought up with excellent backgrounds and a strong sense of personal morality and ethics. Their loan of $1500 was approved quickly, and they didn't give too much thought as to how they'd repay it.

They didn't start paying until a year after graduation. The interest rate was only three percent and they could take as long as ten years to repay. If they became bona fide teachers after getting their degrees, half of the loan would be cancelled. When they had additional need for clothing, car repairs, or other items, the campus loan officer assured them there was plenty of money available for their needs.

Several years and two children later, they enrolled for additional education. Jobs hadn't been as available as they had expected. They kept on borrowing and soon lost track of how much they would have to repay.

After Florence obtained her degree she remained at home to take care of the children. Tom got his master's degree and found a glut of qualified people in the teaching field.

Almost ten years to the day after they had signed their first note for a student loan, Tom took a job as a carpenter's helper.

How could they ever repay their loans with that small income? They toyed with the idea of defaulting or declaring bankruptcy. As quickly as these thoughts entered their minds however, they tossed them aside. They would repay their debts. Each person should assume responsibility for his own actions. They had agreed to borrow the money, not realizing how deeply into debt they were going, so they would repay it. It took them years, but they made it.

Many persons have no qualms about taking bankruptcy as a way out. There are many hardship cases where bankruptcy seems to be justified and other cases where the people involved are simply taking advantage of this easy way out. Rarely is a claim of bankruptcy denied.

The easy way out does not build character. An obligation is an obligation. People should know what they are doing. Strong characters are built through adversity or hardship. Making it easy enfeebles our moral structure in an already weakened society.

GOOD-BYE, DREAM HOUSE

The fateful day arrived. The dream house that Ruth and Joe had built twenty years before had to be sold to satisfy creditors pressing in on every side. It wasn't easy to part with such a home. As Christians, there was no other way for them to go.

The story began when Joe started a construction and property development business.

Things went well as the business expanded in various directions. Some errors in judgment, combined with too quick expansion, found Joe constructing a huge shopping center with little emergency capital. The job was getting nicely under way when a strike was called.

The strike went on and on. The storm began to break. Interim financing was withdrawn. The banks called their loans. Trade creditors, investors, and mortgage companies descended like vultures.

Joe's other enterprises suffered, too. Through the crisis he felt confident that there were sufficient assets to satisfy all the creditors. It was impossible to liquidate these assets in time to meet the various cash demands, however.

Joe and Ruth's Christian faith was their main support through these trying experiences. Their prayers for help brought a new friend, a CPA, who said they had two alternatives.

They could declare corporate as well as personal bankruptcy, which would be the easy way out, or they could meet with all their creditors and try to work out a plan whereby no one would suffer any loss.

The second alternative was the only way they as Christians felt they could go.

The house they loved so much was sold, but the Lord provided them with alternate living accommodations that proved ideal and very inexpensive. They have since been able to liquidate various assets and private company shares gradually to meet all payments as they have come due.

Ruth and Joe found that many of those to whom they owed money in various amounts were also Christians and very sympathetic with their problems. Friendships were made through the experience. There have been many blessings in these new relationships.

What seemed like a tragedy opened new doors.

SHOCKS FOR AN ELECTRICAL CONTRACTOR

Oscar was an electrical contractor in one of the large metropolitan areas of the southwestern United States.

A number of large users of electrical power engaged him to read their meters each month so they could keep an accurate check on the amount of power they were using. He and his wife were the sole owners of their electrical contracting business.

Oscar's company was awarded a job as subcontractor to do the electrical work on a large home. The people for whom this home was being constructed advanced substantial amounts of cash to the prime contractor as the job progressed. In fact, the contractor was paid in full long before the home was completed.

Then it happened. The prime contractor became involved in a number of projects at the same time and was financially wiped out. Work on the home came to an abrupt stop as the subcontractors were not paid for their work.

Every one of the subcontractors was a person of good repute in the area. The news that the prime contractor had gone bankrupt soon spread throughout the city. All of the contractors' reputations were now at stake. The property owners had exhausted their resources and were left with an incomplete home.

Oscar called together the plumber, painter, roofer, and the other subcontractors to determine what they should do. State law gave them the legal right to take over the building. The owners stood to lose all they had paid out to the prime contractor. They had no choice. Oscar felt this was grossly unfair.

Using all of his persuasive powers, he convinced each subcontractor to finish the building, take their losses, and establish themselves in the community as people who conducted their business on a high plane.

Oscar's refusal to take the easy way out carried him through other tough spots. He got an opportunity to bid on a huge street lighting job for the city. He had previously avoided these street lighting jobs.

This time, though, he needed a little more work so he went after this particular job. One of the veterans of city street lighting jobs contacted Oscar.

"I hear that you are going to bid on that street lighting job for the city. You've never bid on any of the previous jobs. Is it true you're in the bidding?"

"Yes. I'd like to have one of those jobs. We are not overly busy just now and I could use that contract to keep my people going."

"You're entitled to that, but let me tell you how we handle these deals. We take turns getting the work. One of us is selected to get the job. He turns in a bid to make a good profit. The rest bid much higher. We'll be glad to let you have a turn, but this time we want you to submit a high bid. Keep your prices up and forget about that job. Your turn will come."

"I couldn't do that. That's collusion, and it is definitely wrong. You could go to jail for that."

"Not a chance. We put nothing in writing. No one could prove a thing."

"Nevertheless, I'll have nothing to do with that sort of a deal."

The competitor left the office wondering what Oscar would do. Oscar decided not to bid on the job. He wanted no part of this illegal procedure. While he himself had not made any agreement as to the price he would submit, he felt it would be very difficult to prove if the matter of collusion ever came to light. His genuine Christian principles said no.

Instead, Oscar decided to go after the electrical contract on the new high school.

It would be a big job and he figured his prices very conservatively as he really wanted to have the winning bid. When all the bids were in, the school board elected to give the job to one prime contractor, a large construction company in the city. They reasoned that this would simplify their work, and they were right.

Oscar went to the prime contractor and submitted his bid for the electrical work. He soon received a call.

"We'd very much like to give you the job. We know your reputation for good work, but your price is about $2000 too high. If you'll reduce your price accordingly to match the lowest bidder, we'd prefer for you to have the job."

"No, I calculated that job very carefully. I need every dollar that I bid. The offer I made is firm."

A few days later, they gave him the job anyway, regardless of his high bid.

Oscar—like Tom and Florence, Ruth and Joe—refused to take the easy way out.

It paid off.

CHAPTER 9

What Are We Responsible For?

THE FINE PRINT SYNDROME

Ever sign something you didn't understand?

Probably. Probably you don't even understand your income tax return. It is the most maligned of all business documents. Efforts to simplify the language of the form seem to add instead to the confusion of the reader.

Rather than try to understand the numerous instructions, many people choose to consult with a specialist presuming, of course, that such a person knows what it is all about and has the correct answers.

Other documents, including insurance policies, contracts, lease agreements, ordinances and regulations, guarantees and warrantees, plus numerous other legal documents with paragraph after paragraph of fine print are also confusing. The average person would readily admit that he has signed such documents without having read through all the terms.

"Even if I did read all the fine print, I still wouldn't understand it," people say. But don't we have a responsibility to know what we're doing?

Along with this situation, there are thousands of laws and rulings intimately related to our daily lives of which we are entirely unaware. We may be violating rules that we never knew existed. We wander innocently into unfamiliar areas totally oblivious of the fact that we are trespassing beyond barriers that are either obscure or completely invisible.

To an unsuspecting person seeking to live within the bounds of the law, the possibility of being guilty without knowing it is frightening. Then to come face to face with the fact that innocence of the law does not excuse anyone really adds to the concern. These are hard judgments to accept. The question then arises in our minds, "What shall we do?"

AN EASY $1000

A member of the board of directors of a very successful corporation was approached by a casual acquaintance with a desire to purchase some stock in the company. The stock of that corporation was closely held, and since the offerings were seldom publicized, the price of the shares was always negotiable. The board member made a promise to the interested party that he would advise her if ever any of the stock became available.

Some time later a minority shareholder of the corporation wanted to dispose of five hundred shares for $8 per share. The board member suddenly remembered the acquaintance who wanted the shares and contacted her. He offered the shares at $10, and the offer was immediately accepted.

That evening the board member mailed a check for $4000 to

the owner of the shares and requested that he send them to him by registered mail, leaving blank the space showing the new owner. The deal was completed and the board member profited to the extent of $1000.

At a subsequent luncheon with his stockbroker the board member did a bit of boasting.

"I picked up an easy $1000 the other day." He then related to the broker the entire incident, and received a chilling response.

The broker informed the board member regarding certain state and federal laws that he had unwittingly broken. If ever his case came to court he would be subjected to heavy fines and possible imprisonment.

This is not an unusual case. We would be amazed at the number of occasions when each of us violates a rule or a law that we never knew existed.

CHRISTIAN CONDUCT

How then are Christians to conduct their lives to avoid such embarrassment?

The vicious part of the whole problem is the fact that many of the pitfalls are placed in the fine print deliberately. They might be classified as escape clauses, but actually a more accurate description of them would be frauds.

Such deceptive statements are so cleverly worded that even a well-informed lawyer or judge is hard pressed to discern the irregularity. The ethical Christian business person would do well to examine his own methods and then alert his customers or clients to the dangers lurking in various transactions.

The complexities of our daily existence are overwhelming.

Lawmakers and bureaucrats are constantly revising statutes and issuing directives, all of which radically alter the behavior of our society.

Christians have a built-in spiritual radar system to alert them to the many dangers in a complex society. Living our lives in a circumspect manner will enable us to avoid some of the cleverly concealed pitfalls. Walking with divine guidance is without question a good course to follow.

However, divine guidance does not excuse us from neglect. Every effort should be made to conform in every way with the rules or laws under which we conduct our affairs.

A LIE IS A LIE, IS A LIE

When the young man in school was asked by his teacher to give a definition for the word *lie* he said,

"A lie is an abomination to the Lord and a very present help in time of trouble."

This may have been the thought in an insurance executive's mind as he related the following story.

"I've been in the insurance business for more than twenty-five years. Because of the nature of our operation, at different times I have had offices located and operating in a number of states.

"At one particular time in my insurance experience I found it expedient to open a brand new office in a state adjoining the one in which I lived. In order to do this I had to get my corporation domesticated in the adjoining state. To do this I had to maintain a physical office in that state for the length of time that I would choose to operate in that state.

"With this in mind and having gone to the state capitol to take the examination necessary for the license, I opened my office in a city that borders both states. As matter of fact, one of the main streets of the city has the state line running through the center—the offices on the north side are in the adjoining state and those on the south side are in the state in which I resided.

"We chose to open our first office several blocks away from this main street. It was to be located in a small shopping center well situated within the boundaries of the other state.

"After maintaining that office, and having some small measure of success in this adjoining state for two or three years, my manager called me on the phone one day and said, 'A brand new office complex has been erected in the city and inasmuch as our lease is about to expire, how about moving the office to the new location?'

"I never really gave the state laws any thought or consideration. I just told him that inasmuch as the rent would be the same and he was going to do all the work in moving the office, he could go right ahead. I would accept and follow his recommendations.

"The time is now about six months later. I had been in our new office on a number of different occasions.

"Then I received a call from the office of Insurance and Banking in this other state asking, 'Is it true that you have moved your office to a new location?'

"At first I could not comprehend why he had asked that question. 'Yes, we have,' I told him. 'I'm sorry that we did not notify you' I said apologetically.

"Then I was completely taken by surprise and shocked

when the fellow asked me, 'Is your new office in our state or is it in your state?' In other words, on which side of the line is the office?

"Suddenly, panic struck. I knew very well that I was now located in my own state rather than the neighboring state where we were required by law to maintain an office. Further, the thought raced through my mind that we have been in violation of the law all these months by operating in a way that would not satisfy the statutes of our adjoining state.

"As these thoughts were running through my mind I was tempted to lie to him. Then, thinking I might not get away with this, I thought I'd tell him that I had to check and let him know. The latter statement would not have been exactly truthful because I knew very well, having been in the office a number of times, that it was, indeed, in my state. The physical location of our office was in no sense of the word in the adjoining state. As these thoughts raced through my mind, I suppose some forty or fifty seconds of silence may have passed by.

" 'Are you still on the line?' the insurance department representative asked me.

"My silence had indicated to him that apparently we were disconnected. 'Yes, I'm still here.' Then I blurted out the truth.

" 'The office is not in your state; it is across the line in the state in which I live.'

"I am not sure why I did not shade the truth or at least stall for some more time during which I might get some legal advice. Perhaps because of the fact that I knew God could never bless any effort to distort the truth. I found myself confessing what I had done. I really thought this would subject me to some severe consequences.

"To my absolute amazement he responded by saying, 'Well, it really doesn't matter on which side of the state line your office is located as long as it is in a border city.'

"Was I ever relieved! To this day I do not know why he asked me this question or why I was faced with this temptation. I suppose the lesson I learned is the one found in Matthew 6:33, 'Seek ye first the kingdom of God, and His righteousness; and all these things will be added unto you.'

"In other words, make an attempt to know your responsibilities and when you do what you know to be right, God will bless you in the long run. We shouldn't pretend that the fine print is beyond our control."

Part Four

LOVE PEOPLE,
USE THINGS

CHAPTER 10

The Ethics of Human Rights

A STEADY CONFLICT

In many ways, the world of business is constantly in conflict with the matter of human rights.

There is a never-ending conflict between employer and employees—the state and its citizens—the ecologist and the land developer.

The objective of the corporation invariably takes precedence over interests or requirements of the employees who make up the organization.

The position of the general manager becomes a difficult one if he wants to treat the employees as people rather than as numbers in a computer.

He realizes any concession on his part, made for personal reasons, might jeopardize his position as manager even to the point of getting him fired.

The profit motive displaces many of the human relationships. Hence, the manager pushes his employees just far enough, stopping just before they protest by demanding higher wages or benefits. In many instances this is a very delicate line.

The paternal attributes of employers are more and more difficult to find.

The dean of a large university noticed a trend of more students taking courses in business administration than in the humanities and remarked to a friend, "Does this indicate on the part of the students, a greater concern for success in business rather than success in living?"

Are human rights in business the forgotten moral concern? As people crystallize problems in human rights overseas or equal rights among women or races, the ethical standards of employee-employer relationships remain very difficult to define.

Just as the investor looks to the corporation for what is considered a fair return on investment, so do employees look to management for an equal share of corporate earnings.

This situation has created a vicious circle of pay increases, followed by higher prices, which, in turn, call for more pay hikes.

The engineer is asked to invent or produce technical improvements to speed up production in order that the higher priced employees will produce more with the same cost as before. The engineer must give no thought to the impact his invention may have on the labor pool. His task is to construct a machine that will keep costs under control.

The next step is to develop a market to enable the corporation to dispose of the product. Easy payment plans and credit card purchases make it easy for wage earners to stretch their credit limits far beyond their ability to pay.

An almost universal reaction is to seek an increase in pay or earnings in order to keep abreast of installment payments. Some people might even resort to bankruptcy. Married couples come to the conclusion that both husband and wife should be gainfully employed to increase family income. This in turn spawns problems at home, increased divorce rates, more unemployment, more dissatisfied people. Many of these people rather than bringing a moral influence to the business world hope to find happiness in the stream of commerce.

One may well argue that to call a halt to industrial accomplishment would be a serious step backward in the development of our society. The nation points with pride to the high standard of living now available to its citizens. At the same time, though, the spiraling cost of modern conveniences is preventing a growing number of people from even buying a home.

As we very correctly consider human rights problems internationally are we neglecting human rights difficulties in business? And if so, who can change the trend?

THE CHALLENGE

On a corporate level, if a paternal relationship between employer and employee is to be established, it must begin with the board of directors or the executive committee. We cannot look to the investors or stockholders to bring the change about. Their prime concern has to do with the operating or balance sheet.

On a personal level human rights must begin within the heart of each individual. There must be a reversal of desires. Selfish desires must give way to those that concern the entire society. Until such a beginning is made by conversion or rebirth, the question of human rights will be without an answer.

The teachings of the Bible affirm that all persons have equal opportunity. There are no exclusions. The rain falls on the just and on the unjust. The sun shines on the good and on the evil. The teachings of Jesus bring us face to face with the responsibilities that we have toward each other as well as to ourselves.

"Therefore all things whatsoever ye would that men should do to you, do ye even so to them." (Matthew 7:12)

On an executive level, business people must be leaders in the effort for human rights. It can be done.

Consider Sir John.

A CONSTRUCTION GIANT

Sir John was one of the greatest construction people in the world. Many honors were conferred on him during his life in construction, the greatest being the job of replacing England's Coventry cathedral, which had been bombed during the war. His construction work was so outstanding that he was knighted by the Queen of England. His firm employed as many as 15,000 persons at one time. They had literally built cities and had done numerous other jobs both large and small including at least a dozen airports.

However, to Sir John business was always secondary. Throughout his long life he always put God first. Although known almost worldwide as a successful business person, Sir John proved the verse:

"Godliness is profitable unto all things, having promise of

the life that now is, and of that which is to come." (I Timothy 4:8)

The key to Sir John's life was his Christian faith, which was intense, simple, and direct. He simply believed what the Bible says. He believed in trying, always and honestly, to do what the Bible tells us to do. Any person who does that will be noticed.

What happens when the Christianity of the Bible becomes involved in the workings of a big modern business?

Sir John's answer was, "Where is the difficulty? There is but one answer to all our problems: one way, one truth, one life. I'm involved with bricks, mortar, and concrete but the Master Builder is God, speaking throughout the Bible.

"To achieve the mastery you must take an act of submission, which means a readiness to accept the truth when you see it and to act on it whether you like the look of it or not: There must be no mental reservation."

In a large establishment employing thousands of people there is always the important matter of employer-employee relations. Sir John's firm had a reputation for getting things done faster with fewer workers.

The people in Sir John's employ were always regarded as people. He contended that as long as management regarded employees simply as economic units, the problems could never be solved.

When each employee was seen as a person, a spiritual being with a unique value in the eyes of his Creator, possessing unique capacities and needs, the problems would solve themselves.

This is true human rights. People are all members of a

community. The body depends on its members and the members on the body. In other words, there must be team spirit.

This is an easy phrase but Sir John determined to work this out in practical detail for his employees just as he had done with his own life. His solution produced results because everyone took note of the practical details and understood the spirit behind them.

Sir John set up reforms and benefits for his employees, in many ways pioneering entirely new advantages for workers.

He understood his responsibilities toward good human rights in business and took action.

DAVID—A LEADER IN BUSINESS HUMAN RIGHTS

David was the vice-president of a large finance company (166 branches), a position he got after twenty-eight years of loyal service.

During the first two decades of David's career with the company he had enjoyed good success, with a series of ten promotions. His firm Christian stand was well known throughout the company.

Management thought of him as a people-oriented "go getter" who led with team spirit, knowing that decent people liked to pull their weight.

During the early years, it had become apparent to the company that selection, training, motivation, and retention were the basic keys to a successful team. It took tactful and right timing to weed and prune the team of those who were not performing. Management came to realize that:

1. Young men like titles

2. 30- and 40-year-olds need money

3. Those over 50 like peace

The staff grew steadily with three assistant vice-presidents, thirteen field supervisors, and a manager for each branch.

Eventually David was put in charge of all 166 branch offices. The honors came in. He was given the "President's Award," the highest award in the company, and was elected to the board of governors. He was also elected to the board of two of the company subsidiaries—one in Canada, the other in Bermuda.

David's performance had earned him the awards. His division had the best employee retention of any of the eighteen departments in the company throughout North America, Australia, and England.

These were great years. Although travel commitments were extremely heavy, David held two offices in the local church and enjoyed a happy home life with his wife and two children. David got one raise after another, along with increased responsibilities—plus the friendship, appreciation, and respect of the president and board members.

Then storm clouds began to gather. New leadership took over at company headquarters, complete with a "non-people," "hard-nosed" stance.

New policies implemented by written directives were sent out without consultation or even test periods.

"Such procedure," said the new management, "would take too long. Tell your people what to do and make them do it."

This philosophy, combined with an impossible and untenable leadership, brought many difficult problems to David's division.

Paternalism was shoved to one side if not disregarded altogether. Employees began to feel like numbers in a computer. Soon personalities were lost in the relentless drive for more and greater profits.

David protested and was challenged from day to day. The new ruthless methods of top leadership did not blend with the teachings of the Word of God. The new materialistic motivation moved relentlessly without regard for customer or employee goodwill.

Although inflation was in double-digit figures, management limited salary increases to a mere five percent.

One by one excellent members of the staff and the branch managers resigned. David couldn't persuade them to remain. He no longer believed in the company principles and actions. But David was at peace. This was not really his company. He didn't own it. The board of directors and the executive committee could operate it as they saw fit, but he would voice his objections regardless.

David soon realized that he couldn't even live with that viewpoint. He was a problem to management's expeditious ways. They didn't need his conscience to interfere with their methods. If he stayed with the company, he'd have to become a soldier and follow commands without giving them much thought. Still he tried reasoning and persuasion. He also tried ignoring the objectionable principles.

But he couldn't. He finally decided to resign.

"Ride it out," his friends advised. "Times and personnel change. Policies will be modified."

He would be giving up a lot if he resigned—twenty-eight years of seniority, an excellent seasoned staff of three vice-presidents, thirteen field supervisors, 166 office managers, an exceptional secretary of fifteen years, and a salary with benefits equivalent to $65,000. At the same time, he was six years from an early pension, had no job prospects, and would experience a sudden let-up from the demanding schedule and responsibilities of an executive.

Also, business journals were warning against change in this specific year. Statistics gave clear evidence of the challenge facing any person seeking employment—especially those over 45.

David resigned anyway. With proper notice and a special letter of thanks to all who had worked with and for him, he left. His parting words to the president and executive committee members:

"I will go out and seek people of my own kind with whom to work." That statement was to be well honored.

Without the responsibilities of a huge enterprise, David sought for something to occupy his time. He had no ideas, no plans. So he enrolled in a Bible school to increase his knowledge of the Word of God. Through the summer months he burned the midnight oil to obtain credits on such subjects as New Testament theology, Christian apologetics, church history, and the church in society.

The rewarding struggle not only fully occupied his capacities but confirmed his decision to quit the job.

While studying, he sent his resume to an executive placement agency. Shortly afterward, he was offered a high position with a large trust company. Without knowing the offer, another friend advised David of the same opportunity.

He investigated and found that two of the three top

executives were Christians. The exception was the president, who thought that three born-again people in top spots was probably not a good thing.

"But, I'll hire you David, if you don't make your beliefs too evident."

Red flags all over the place. David shared his concern with the president. His Christian beliefs formed the basis for his management principles. He couldn't do without them.

"Maybe you ought to reconsider," he told the president.

"I'll call you on this, David."

Would the position be given to him or not? Agencies were loaded with people looking for just such positions. The anxiety did not last long. The next day the phone rang. It was the president of the trust company calling.

"The job is yours, David—and no interference with your Christian testimony."

Sir John and David. Two men who know something can be done about the problem of human rights in business.

CHAPTER 11

Employees

PAYING EMPLOYEES WHAT THEY ARE WORTH

Ask any person if he's getting paid a just equitable salary, for his job, and almost always that person will say no.

Industry recognizes this fact and tends to keep the rate of pay just a trifle below what it should be. The argument: Every employee must show a profit.

Stanley was a skilled mechanic. He asked his supervisor for an increase since he'd made the company a lot of money. Surprisingly, the supervisor agreed and granted the mechanic an increase in pay. As the mechanic turned to go back to his work, the supervisor said:

"Just a minute. Of course, you will do your best from now on."

"No," said Stanley. "I can't afford that. Even with your increase I'm still not paid what I'm worth."

EVEN THE BRANCH MANAGER TOOK A CUT

Don's first job with the company came during a period of hard times. The company announced a pay cut for all employees. Even the department manager received a salary cut. Since Don's responsibility included some accounting, he was working with financial records. He discovered that his immediate supervisor more than made up for his cut of $100 per month by turning in grossly inflated expense account vouchers. He encouraged Don to do the same. When Don refused, tension developed.

This was Don's first brush with the unethical handling of salaries.

Then he got promoted to Salt Lake City, where he would be the branch manager. A good raise was promised.

Don and his family moved right after Christmas. He dropped by his old office to get some records and say good-bye to his boss.

"Oh, by the way, Don, I just received a memo from the head office. They only approved one-third of the promised increase."

Don was stunned. He had attended a farewell party. His furniture was on the way to the new location. Sadly, he went to the car and looked for words to explain to his wife about the broken promises.

They went on their way, not rejoicing but looking ahead to new experiences.

The new office prospered. Within two years, it was number one in all three operating categories. Don received recognition in the form of commendatory letters. Still the financial rewards did not come.

As a Christian, he knew workers should be paid according to their efforts and achievements. Don had always felt that management has the responsibility to evaluate the employee and recognize his value to the company by paying him fairly. In twelve years he had never asked for an increase but had written to the head office frequently to recommend raises for his employees. They were always approved.

The boss flew out from the head office to ask Don to be branch manager of a larger office on the West Coast. Don's feelings were mixed. Here was a new and greater opportunity back in California, but he had enjoyed Utah. He noticed that no salary figure had been given. So he asked.

"You'll have greater opportunity for incentive bonuses, but your base salary won't be adjusted until the end of the year. That's customary, as you know."

But Don didn't see any reason to move and told his boss, who was startled by the decision.

"But, all the plans have been made and we assumed you would make the move because it was good for the company."

"I'm sorry. I'll stay here."

The boss took the offensive, telling Don his attitude showed lack of cooperation and was tantamount to resigning. It's really something to see to what lengths a corporation man will go to enforce his will.

Don tendered his resignation and was asked to reconsider. In thirty days it was final.

Don got another, better job with a different company. In his new responsibilities, he constantly reviews and evaluates employees, giving them increases voluntarily.

"People who help to produce business are paid salaries exceeding those paid by competitors plus quarterly profit-sharing bonuses. I want no employee to have to ask for a raise. The formula works. The business is successful," says Don.

PIRACY IN INDUSTRY

The practice of hiring talented help away from a similar enterprise or competitor has been going on for centuries. It seems that the one who does the theft considers himself a conqueror of sorts. Sometimes the motive is to find out more about a competitive process or product. At other times, it is to secure a person with exceptional skills. The inducements vary considerably: higher remuneration or salary, stock options, special fringe benefits, pleasant working conditions.

Companies that lose employees to competitors are often guilty of the same practice themselves. The general manager of a large firm with huge government contracts lost one of his key men to a competitor. He later boasted that he had retaliated by hiring away sixteen employees from that same thieving competitor.

GOODBYE, WELDERS

Oliver, the superintendent of a modest-sized manufacturing company reported a flagrant act of piracy. His organization had made a breakthrough in some of its stainless steel equipment.

Oliver and his associates developed their own welding rod and a process for using it. They were highly successful in the construction of welded stainless steel equipment.

One day, two men called on the president of Oliver's company. They represented an industry engaged in the manufacture of railroad cars and similar equipment. They were anxious to learn how to work with stainless steel and wondered if they could in any way be permitted to see how it was done. After a brief conference the president approved the visit.

The men returned the following day and spent most of the time with the key men in the welding department.

The next Monday morning Oliver didn't have a stainless steel welder in his factory. His entire crew had been hired away by the railroad equipment company at substantial increases in salary.

Often the piracy of skilled help is a very expensive matter for the organization that is raided. One manufacturer producing a highly specialized line of equipment reports that the cost of training a replacement may exceed a quarter of a million dollars.

The intangible losses cannot be priced. Yet this practice is condoned by many reputable organizations and is not limited to any one particular industry.

It is hardly Christian, however.

NEED FOR A GOOD EXAMPLE

The president of a mulitnational corporation sat in the board room surrounded by the directors of the company. His face was stern and he seemed rather ill at ease.

One of the directors, studying the appearance of the president, asked, "What's the trouble? You look as if the whole world has caved in on top of you today."

"That's exactly the way I feel. I really don't know what is happening out there in our factory. During the past six weeks or so we have had more complaints from customers than we have received in two years.

"They're complaining about defects, breakdowns, poor deliveries, poor service, and a host of other things. This is not a good situation and it is rather distressing. I cannot understand why, all of a sudden, we are swamped with all this dissatisfaction on the part of our customers."

"Well," said the director, "maybe God is answering prayers. Do you believe in prayer?"

"Of course I do. Whatever made you ask that?"

The director calmly replied, "I got here a bit early this morning for our meeting and decided to take a stroll through the shop.

"As I passed the different gangs of workers in the various departments, I heard them praying. Well, maybe I shouldn't really call it prayer.

"They were calling out, 'God damn this and God damn that.' It wasn't just once but over and over again in group after group. If the men keep calling on God to condemn something, it may be that, unknown to them, He is answering their prayers. Maybe if the men were asking the Lord to bless the machines, we wouldn't be having these problems."

For what seemed an age not a word was said by any of the members of the board. The director had made his point. Sure, he had carried it to an extreme. But it points out the importance of a final point about employee relations. Good examples are so important. If leadership hadn't been using the expletives neither would the workers.

VICTIM OF A FIRE

A tragedy struck the home of a poor family in the pine forests of northern Wisconsin. Three small children were rescued but fire claimed the lives of the parents. Kind neighbors decided, since there were no known relatives, they would divide the children among them. Espen, a guide for hunters and fishermen, took the four-year-old boy and was shocked with the boy's language. He knew more vile language than any person Espen had ever known. A fisherman gave Espen advice:

"I'll tell you what to do. Just leave the kid alone. Don't whip him or even threaten him. Since neither you nor your wife use that kind of language, he will soon forget all his cuss words and speak just like you do."

The system really worked. The little lad soon dropped the bad language and spoke just like his new parents.

If the fellows at the top would quit swearing, the men beneath them would soon drop that kind of speech as well. If the executives are honest, it will encourage the rest of the employees to be honest.

Example is at the heart of good employer-employee relationships.

CHAPTER 12

Love God
Also

NOW I'D like to tell you my story, for it supports every claim made in this book. It vindicates the viewpoint that God's ethics are the best.

Moving into an entirely new business venture often brings with it a grave sense of doubt. Is this a wise choice to make? Have I really counted the cost? When the tide turns and the decision is vindicated, a warm feeling of satisfaction replaces the doubts and once again peace reigns in the heart.

As an engineer who had spent many years in the food processing industry, I had never thought that some day I would find myself owning a retail religious bookstore. Being a lover of books, I had often visited a certain Christian bookstore, sometimes to browse but more often to buy a volume or two. The staff at the store, as well as the manager, greeted me warmly each time I came to buy or just to look around.

One day the manager, who was getting old and weary of it all, surprised me by asking if I would like to buy the store. I promptly replied that the food processing engineering field and Christian book retailing were really miles apart, not at all compatible. I'd be out of my mind to even consider the matter.

Being a persistent person, the bookstore manager did not give up very easily. She suggested that inasmuch as I was an avid reader and loved good books, the store would be an ideal place for me to spend my retirement years.

After several subsequent visits to the store with similar prodings by the manager, I told my wife about the proposition. Her response was,

"Let's pray about it. Maybe the Lord wants you to take over the place."

So we did just that, we prayed about it.

The next time the manager of the bookstore repeated her suggestion I said, "I really have no intention of giving up my present position, but if I could find a good manager to run the place for me, I might consider buying it."

My wife had a brother-in-law who was a top-notch salesperson but who knew nothing about retailing religious books. Although he was a Christian, his business interests were confined to selling water pumps for irrigation projects. I discussed the matter with him over the phone and wondered if he would be interested in managing the place if I bought it?

He admitted to knowing nothing about retailing books but indicated that he would be willing to give it a try. However, before he could move his family a thousand miles, he would have to sell his home.

The very next day he phoned me to say that his home had

been sold and finished the conversation by saying: "You've just hired yourself a bookstore manager."

Up to that point I had not entered into any negotiations to buy the store.

The events of the next few days moved along rapidly. An investigation of the business at the bookstore revealed that it was in a horrible mess. The liabilities were at least as much as the place was worth. Accounts payable were delinquent to a point where creditors were pressing hard for payment of accounts. Purchases were almost all on a C.O.D. basis. Sales had been drifting lower each month, with losses climbing at an even more rapid pace. Inventory was very low.

The picture did not look good. The wise course to take would have been to walk away and forget the whole thing. In fact, that is just what my banker advised me to do. Opposed to this was the fact that this was the only independent Christian bookstore for many miles around. Many Christians depending on it for good books and religious supplies would have been keenly disappointed and dismayed to see the store go out of business.

We bombarded ourselves with all sorts of reasons why we should take over the business. After all, a healthy infusion of cash would satisfy the suppliers and replenish the depleted inventory. Good business methods with aggressive selling would soon lift the store out of the red and into the black. At least, so we reasoned.

The newly appointed manager and I decided to pension the previous manager, rewarding her for many years of loyal service, and then move along with a fresh start. That is just what we did.

Then the problems began. Suppliers swooped down on us

like vultures demanding that their accounts be brought up to date before further shipments would be made. Promises made by certain publishers to go along and help us to get going were completely forgotten by them. The picture was not good. Securities were sold and bank accounts drained in the hope that things would soon change for the better. We determined not to seek help from friends although many of them were more than willing to come to our rescue.

We decided that any losses would be our own. If we went down the drain, we did not want to take anyone along with us. After all, we felt that the Lord had directed us into this thing and our confidence was in Him.

The staff cooperated beautifully. There was a determination on the part of each one to make the business succeed. Gradually the losses shrank. Pressures eased up. Soon the figures changed from red to black. Old customers returned as the shelves once again stocked their requirements. Progress was slow but encouraging. The business seemed to have at last settled down into a smooth operation.

One day my secretary called across the desk, "There's a lawyer on the phone. He says he must talk to you."

I picked up the phone wondering what this was all about.

"Hello," the voice said. "Are you the president of the bookstore?"

"Yes, I am."

"Is it still in business?"

"Yes, it is."

"Are you in good standing with the state as a corporation?"

"Yes, but tell me," I asked, "what is this all about? Am I being sued by anyone? Why are you asking me all these questions?"

"I'll gladly tell you why. A client of mine died very

suddenly. In reviewing her will I find that she has left her entire estate to the president of the bookstore. You are that person, aren't you?"

"Yes, but who is the lady who has remembered me so kindly?"

The lawyer mentioned her name and probably expected me to register some kind of shock at her sudden death.

After a short period of silence he said, "Of course, you knew her."

"No, I'm sorry to say, I've never heard the name before."

"And yet she left you her entire estate," he responded.

"Well," I asked, "what does the estate amount to? Just a few hundred dollars? Is it worth driving 150 miles?"

"Wait a minute," he interrupted. "It's thousands of dollars."

"Great," I replied. "I'll come right down to see you."

"Better bring your lawyer with you," he suggested.

We went on to set up a date for a meeting to determine what had to be done to settle the estate. Within a few days, my attorney and I journeyed downstate to meet with the woman's lawyer. He revealed that the estate consisted of a modest home with its furniture, a new car in the garage, a mortgage on a chicken ranch, a number of government bonds in a safety deposit box, and a nice sized savings account.

The lawyer then tried to explain this unusual will. It had been written some fifteen years earlier and no later will could be found. He then asked me who the president of the corporation was at that time the will was first drawn. When I told him, his next question was:

"Is he still alive?"

"No, he passed away many years ago."

The whole affair seemed as incredible to the lawyer as it did to me. He sat in his chair and just stared at me with a puzzled look on his face. I broke the spell when I asked how soon I could take possession of all that property.

At that point, the two lawyers got into a discussion regarding the legal aspects of the situation. An advertisement had to be placed in several papers and continued for a period of six weeks. At the end of that time, if no one had appeared to protest the will, we would meet in court for final disposition of the matter.

Instead of advertising for six weeks, we suggested carrying the advertisement for eight weeks. This was done but no protests were received. It appeared that the deceased had had no living relatives. Her husband had died some years before the date of the will.

The time set for the court hearing was just two days before Christmas. When we arrived at the courthouse, my attorney and I noticed that our case was the second on the calender for that afternoon. The court clerk came to us and told us that the judge wanted to move our case to the last place on the calendar instead of the second one. He had reasons for this which he would explain later. The delay would possibly be two hours long but since we had waited eight weeks already, two hours did not seem very long. We consented.

Soon all the other cases before the court were settled. Just a few of us remained in the courtroom: the judge, the bailiff, the court clerk, the coroner, the attorney for the county, my attorney, and I. I was asked to take the stand and was duly sworn in.

The judge turned to me with a pleasant smile and said, "I

apologize for delaying your case. You see, this is my last day on the bench. When we settle our business here today I'll be retired. But this case seemed to me to be most interesting. I want you to tell me the whole story behind this bookstore.

"Why, your Honor," I said, "that would take a half hour or more."

"All right," he replied. "You waited patiently all afternoon, I can carry on another half hour. Give me the story, I want to hear it."

For the next half hour I related all the events leading up to that very time in his court; how the Lord seemed to lead my wife and me into taking over this business; the discouragements and doubts that followed; and then its gradual emergence into a fairly stable organization. The judge listened patiently. When I completed my discourse, he stopped weaving his chair back and forth from side to side and, leaning down toward me, he said, "You know what I am going to do with you? I'm going to make you the sole beneficiary and the sole executor of this estate."

"Thank you very much, Judge," I said, "but tell me what all that means in layman's language."

"It means that it is all yours and you can do as you please with it. You don't have to answer to anyone, not even me."

With that, he signed the papers and handed them over to me. I studied them for a while and then turning to the judge I said, "Your honor, this is incredible. The total value of the estate AS SHOWN BY THE CORONER AND THE COUNTY ATTORNEY IS ALMOST THE EXACT AMOUNT TO THE DOLLAR THAT MY WIFE AND I HAVE INVESTED IN THIS BUSINESS. The Lord has given back to us every dollar that we risked to carry on His business."

The judge had one final remark.

"I suppose," he said, "that you and your wife will buy a nice new car and then take a trip to Europe."

"No, your Honor," I replied, "we will just double the size of the business." Then he wished me a merry Christmas.

There is a sequel to the story that seems incredible. The county attorney advised that there would be a tax on the estate payable to the state. I agreed that he should pay this from funds in the bank. Several months later the state returned the amount of the tax in full, stating that inasmuch as this was a religious bookstore, all estate taxes would be waived.

I—like all the men and women in this book—have found that to love God is the first rule in ethics. There are many other principles, but to love God is where you start.